God, Don't You Care?

Answering the Question You Didn't
Know You Asked

By Chelsey Dollman

Title: God, Don't You Care?
Subtitle: Answering the Question You Didn't Know You Asked

Copyright © 2020 Chelsey Dollman. All rights reserved.

Cover Art: Chelsey Dollman
Editor: Marijka Neal

Canadian laws and regulations are public domain and not subject to copyright. Any unauthorized copying, reproduction, translation, or distribution of any part of this material without permission by the author is prohibited and against the law.

ISBN-13: 9781777389710

Table of Contents

Chapter 1   **Asking the Question You Didn't Know You Had**

Chapter 2   **Am I a "Bad" Christian if I Struggle?**

Chapter 3   **The Root of Bitterness**

Chapter 4   **Leave Reasoning Behind**

Chapter 5   **Comparison is a Killer**

Chapter 6   **Healing from the Past**

Chapter 7   **When You Least Expect It**

Chapter 8   **Authenticity and Transparency in Struggle**

Chapter 9   **I'm in the Middle of It, Now What?**

Chapter 10   **Don't Stuff Those Feelings**

Chapter 11 **Trusting, Still**

Chapter 12 **Resting While You Wait**

Chapter 13 **Proof That God Cares (In Case You Didn't Know)**

This book is dedicated to the quiet and meek souls, who pray in the early hours, bowing at the altar, seemingly unnoticed, but are a rock in the faith. To those who patiently endure hardships, yet are always quick to pray and encourage others who struggle. To the souls who are hiking up the Everest of their faith, running the race, yet not flinching when asked to carry on their back another soul in need. To those who may seem on the outside as a mouse, yet on the inside their faith roars like a lion, confident in Him from whom their help comes.

CHAPTER 1

Asking the Question You Didn't Know You Had

It was a normal day, just like any other. I had dropped the kids off at school and as usual, I went for my morning hike. I love to hike during that time because it is when I feel like I walk and talk with God. But before I tell you about that heart-changing hike, let me back up a little.

I had been struggling with some health issues for nearly a year and it seemed like nothing was getting better; in fact, it seemed like they were compiling. One of those issues was knee pain from an accident the previous year. I was thankful most of the time because I was still able to walk. I was very much aware of that and grateful. But I was also frustrated that after one year of praying for healing, my knee wasn't any better.

It wasn't just my knee though. I was also dealing with a more serious issue with my health that had been dragging on for seven years, and I had been calling out to God asking for mercy to change the situation. At one point it all came to a head and the doctor told me I had to deal with the issue sooner than later and it wasn't what I wanted to hear. I felt trapped, like an animal cornered in a pen. He laid out three options but none of them were ideal. I wanted another option to open up. I wanted option number four. I wanted a miracle!

With my whole heart, mind and soul, I prayed day and night for a miracle for over ten months. It was all I could think about. It consumed my mind. But the clock was running out on which option I had to choose. I resisted choosing any option because I kept hoping for a miracle.

The day finally came when I had to make a decision, and I was mad. I was hurting. I was scared. I felt like I wanted to crawl under a rug and come out when it was all over. But I couldn't. After praying for many months, and lots of discussion with my husband, we chose one of the three options. It seemed like the best choice out of all three, although I was deeply aching with disappointment that I hadn't received a miraculous healing. I kept praying and hoping for a miracle every day.

A month later, the day finally came when I had to undergo the procedure. It was fairly quick. But it was also scary and stressful. God definitely gave me the grace to have some semblance of peace amidst the storm, that day. The process took an entire day but at the end, I was glad it was over and I was grateful to God, knowing that He gave me the grace to endure it. I know healing can come in all forms and I was open to receiving what God had for me, even if it meant He was was working through the doctors. All throughout that day, I could feel God giving me the strength to endure what I had to endure.

The truth is, the storm was really the ten months leading up to the procedure, more than it was the procedure itself. In that time, it was a daily battle to keep my mind on God, trusting Him to guide me and to keep my hope up that He was going to bring me through this storm. I wanted Him to show up and perform a 'suddenly' in my life. You know: 'suddenly' take away the struggle, 'suddenly' be miraculously healed; 'suddenly' be free of this issue.

It was probably the hardest season of my life but through it all, God gave me so many confirmations of His hand upon me, His guidance of my steps and the confidence that He was taking care of me. Although they were some of the hardest months of my life, they were also the most spiritually intimate months of my life. In so many moments, I felt God as close to me as the air I breathed. It's something that I continue to cherish. As well, in that time period, I experienced two miraculous touches from God (a physical healing in my stomach that was a five year battle, as well as an angelic miracle, saving me from a terrible crash) that blessed me and encouraged me. Sometimes the victories God has in store for us are not the victories we would have expected, but they are victories nonetheless!

> *In so many moments, I felt God as close to me as the air I breathed.*

During that hard season, when I was right in the middle of the struggle, my knee problem started from a motor biking accident. Now, it wasn't even that the knee problem was that big of a deal. It was uncomfortable, but far less problematic and extreme as the other health issue. The problem was, I was already feeling worn out emotionally from the larger health battle. Knee pain was the last thing I wanted to deal with after having just gone through a deep valley, and now here I was, walking through another valley, and asking God for a miracle. I tried to keep perspective on the situation, comparing it to those who are in much more dire and difficult situations, yet it didn't make me feel any better. My pain was real. My struggle was real. It didn't matter what someone else was going though, this was *my struggle* and it was tormenting me. Why did it appear that I had all these storms in my life and others were walking through life without even so much as a tiny cloud in sky?

That was the lead-up to the place that I was in, emotionally and spiritually, as I set out for a hike that day. I didn't realize that one of the emotions I felt during that hard, ten-month season, and leading up to that particular hike day was that of anger. I was angry about the struggle in which I found myself. I was angry that I hadn't been miraculously healed and had to undergo the procedure I dreaded the previous month. I was angry because I felt like God had left me—alone in the mess. I, myself, was not even aware that I was harbouring these feelings.

As I was hiking, I was praying about the situation with my knee, and sharing with God how frustrated I was with it. I began to realize that I had gone from pleading with God for months, to now being impatient and almost angry with Him that He hadn't yet answered my request. I started to think about why I deserved healing for my knee. I started to count up all the reasons why I had 'earned' it; I questioned the verses about healing, the verses about asking and receiving, and I asked why that hadn't happened for me.

There was a buildup of months and months of unexpressed and unrealized emotions, and all of the sudden they began to spill out of me, like a pot of water that breaches the edge and spills out onto the hot burner. It was as if I was a can of soda, shaken vigorously, spewing out unstoppably. Once the seal was broken, I couldn't stop the contents from forcing their way out. My emotions began to burst from their dormant home, pushing aside anything in their way as I began to pour my heart out to God. I had opened the floodgates. I could not stop them. I had tried to suppress them, tried to ignore them; I had tried to be an exemplary, 'good soldier' but I was wrestling with giants that I did not know how to contend with. I had been fooling myself for the last ten months in believing that I wasn't angry with the outcome. I had smiled and said in agreement with others, "Yes, I'm doing okay," while inside I knew my speech was fraudulent. I was trying to 'keep it together' for everyone around me in that season as I faced the mountain before me, but inside I was broken, sliced into a thousand pieces, with no capability within myself to put them back together. Yet, for those many months I didn't acknowledge or accept my feelings because they somehow felt taboo, wrong—ungrateful.

With each physical step I took, I felt myself behaving like a toddler in the middle of a temper-tantrum. My pace quickened and my steps thudded more angrily as I pushed along. I could feel myself nearly stomping my feet with each passing step, but consciously unaware I was doing so. Louder and stronger my thuds became, quicker and swifter my pace increased. I had reasoned in my mind that it was owed to me, without even being aware that I had been harbouring these feelings: *'How could He let me go through the first struggle, and now this, too? He could step in! He could have healed me ten months ago, but He didn't. Why didn't He? He could immediately heal my knee now, and I'd be done with this! He could!'* I began to say to myself.

All of the sudden—seemingly out of nowhere—a question bubbled to the surface of my mind. It was like an impatient air bubble released from its slumber—racing from the sludgy bottom of the pond towards the light. Helpless to recognize that it was already upon me, it forced its way to the top and before I could stop it, it burst out of me like a champagne cork: "God, don't you care?"

I told myself, that I was—after all—doing Kingdom work, doing His will, being a good soldier. Doing. Doing. Doing. Didn't God want to reward me for all I was doing? But when did 'doing' ever become part of the equation? Did I believe that if I did enough 'good works' that God would owe me? Wait…what?

I came to a halt. Stopped in the middle of the path between earth and sky, I stood still. I started recalling the past number of thoughts as they spiralled down a bitter path through my mind. They stung my heart. It was as if the Holy Spirit paused my mind for a moment and almost as if I was a third party looking at my heart, I saw a glimpse of my impatience, selfishness and ignorance…not to mention lack of trust and entitlement. Had I really believed what I just thought? Was I really basing my thoughts on works, or worse, on believing God owed me? Did I really believe I was entitled to tell God what to do? I fell inside. I had gone from requesting healing for my knee to demanding it. I don't know when the switch happened. It was subtle and it was over time. It came upon me like a winter fog drifting into a sunken valley, filling crevices and blanketing the earth with its wispy mist.

I realized that I had been cycling thoughts of entitlement for months, unaware. I was struck by my own lack of awareness, my lack of transparency with self and with God. I fell on my proverbial face and I was immediately overcome with emotions of utter shame and disbelief that I had been letting my mind wander there, realistically for weeks, maybe even months, subtly letting these thoughts creep into my mind. How could I? Here I was, completely blessed in so many ways, far too many to count, and yet I was complaining about the one or two things that I wanted God to change, with no regard for His awe, reverence or timing. With no regard for the amount of control I was trying to implement on what He should do. I guess I thought I knew better.

It was one of the hardest realizations of which I've been made aware in my walk with God. I felt almost naked, exposed, embarrassed—perhaps how Adam and Eve felt when they recognized their nakedness in the garden. I was angry at myself for ever being angry at the God of goodness who I love and adore. Many times in my life I had heard stories of people who struggled with something that made them angry with God; in my arrogance, I never counted myself as one of those people. Yet…I was aware now that I, in fact, was one of those people, too.

Ashamed of my behaviour, I immediately repented and asked for God to forgive me. I wanted to shed the layers of my sin like a snake who slithers out of his old scales, writhing and twisting to free himself. The immediate emotions that followed that next hour were of guilt, shame and utter wretchedness. Instead of feeling freed, and being thankful that the Holy Spirit had spoken truth into my life, I allowed my own insecurity and emotions to make me feel so little. Instead of being rooted in knowing that once I had repented and asked forgiveness, I was forgiven, I alternately went down a path of feeling wretched. *'How could I ever feel that way towards God? How could I be so selfish? Who am I to think I know better than God?'*

As I continued on my hike, I just kept thinking about how ashamed I was of myself…then all of the sudden I felt a great peace wash over me. It was big, as if a large blanket had been wrapped around me. I felt God reminding me that He forgives me and loves me, in spite of myself. I felt Him telling me that I didn't have to beat myself up—that His Son already accomplished that on the cross. I could, instead, walk in His forgiveness. I also needed to forgive myself. His gift to me that day was giving me awareness of my thoughts, and allowing me to accept the feelings I had been harbouring. I couldn't hide from them anymore—I needed to expose them before God and really lay down my pride, and be honest about the feelings and emotions I was grappling with. The beauty in what God was doing through revealing that I needed to address my feelings, was that He didn't condemn or shame me when I laid them at His feet. He simply reminded me that it's okay to be angry with the circumstances. It's okay to be honest with Him about how we feel. He loves it and encourages us to be open with Him. He is all-knowing, yet acknowledging how we feel is an important part of intimacy with God. The questioning and the feelings are not sinful—but allowing them to go unresolved is.

Rather than me ignoring my feelings for all those months, God would have loved to speak into them. I thought by ignoring and stuffing my feelings way down deep inside, I was doing God a favour. I thought by doing so, I was being a 'good daughter'—being obedient. I thought I would offend God by asking Him the questions I wrestled with. I assumed that it would sadden God to tell him I was upset, angry, hurt. I wanted to spare Him from the feelings of bitterness that were taking root in my heart. But I overlooked something—He already knew. He already saw the rips in my heart and He wanted me to let Him in to help sew them up so that they didn't turn into scars.

But I wasn't willing. I was proud. I was embarrassed that I wasn't strong enough to shoulder it on my own. I assumed that if I didn't acknowledge my hurt, it would just go away. I assumed that if I didn't speak of it or acknowledge my frustration, anger and hurt to God, He wouldn't feel betrayed. I felt that if I expressed these feelings out loud, I would have—just like Peter—betrayed and denied my Lord. That stung me—deeply.

But God did something that surprised me—He began to show me where He was during those ten months of stress. He didn't make me feel ashamed but He instead brought me back, in my mind, to the day of the procedure, and to the many days when I was in my room, crying out in prayer. He showed me how He was there each time—holding my hand or wiping my tears. He was with me—I wasn't alone. I know it can feel lonely in the struggle sometimes, because we can't see God physically, but as God promises, He never leaves or forsakes us (Hebrews 13:5).

He reminded me for the next few hours, days and weeks of His great love, and just how *big* His love is and how much He loves me! I kept hearing Him say, "My banner over you is love" (Song of Solomon 2:4). It was like a blanket that He wrapped me in. I even remember waking up one night and spiritually seeing an actual banner over my head and our bed. I felt so hedged in (Psalm 91) and protected by His love. He showed me that I didn't need to hide my feelings from Him. He showed me where I needed to repent and ask forgiveness. But it was so gentle each time.

No lie of the enemy was going to continue to penetrate my mind because God's love was protecting me. The only way to cast out fear is with perfect love (1 John 4:18). That verse had always perplexed me until that day, when all the sudden it became so clear. He wasn't going to allow fear to enter, and so His love cast out the fear for me. It was such a beautiful example of His love and something that has really transformed the way that I receive His love for me.

What astounds me is that He took a situation where I really could have been reprimanded but in His mercy He poured out His great love. This is a principle of God's character that astounds me each time. That doesn't mean that I didn't repent and that God didn't show me how to proceed going forward, but it was still a beautiful example of how God extends mercy to grace to us in our time of need.

Learning through experience

My story, while practical and a good example of God's mercy and grace, is very different to read than it is to experience. As a writer, I've tried to bring you into as much understanding of the emotions and feelings as I can. I've tried to help you imagine what it might have felt like for me. But it's still not the same as experiencing it yourself.

What if you've been angry and frustrated with God and you haven't reached that point of self-awareness or letting Him in, yet? Or perhaps you haven't even come to the point of acknowledging your feelings to God. Before you go any further, it's time to ask yourself the question: What feelings have I been ignoring that I need to bring before God? It is in those seasons of struggle when we can easily misplace our frustration towards God instead of realizing He is always our solution to every problem. Struggle can often lead to bitterness and resentment. We get impatient and we think that all our problems should just go away immediately once we pray about them. And sometimes they do! After all, God is the God of miracles. But when they don't resolve immediately, often the enemy comes in and plants seeds of doubt, worry, anger, frustration, confusion, entitlement and so many other things. The enemy does not want to see your struggle build your faith, he wants it to tear your faith down.

The pain in my knee was the last straw in the sense that it was what set off the chain of events that led me to realization of my hurt —but it wasn't the root of the issue. The issue was in my heart and it took the problem with my knee for me to get to the end of myself and be open to hearing the Holy Spirit reveal the truth in my heart. That's what God is interested in most: healing our hearts, and having communion and a clean slate between God and us.

Even as I write this, my knee is still not 100%…but I know that one day it will be. Even if it's not this side of heaven, God is taking care of me and I know as I trust in Him, I am not only building my faith but I allowing Him to be 100% in charge of the situation. Who better to be taking care of my problems? Even from the moment I began to write this book, until now, my knee has dramatically improved. I would say it's very close to 100% healed and I have no doubt that it's God's work.

If you aren't sure where you land in the spectrum of questioning God, take a moment and pray. Ask Him to reveal to you if this an area of struggle. My guess is that you wouldn't have been drawn to this book if you weren't grappling with this question of God's care for you in some way. I'm here to encourage you though, that you are not alone. You do not need to feel shame or condemnation for your feelings. Remember that God convicts, not condemns. God brings restoration, not shame. God knows your thoughts and He's ready to answer your questions. Don't waste ten months, like I did, ignoring what was going on in my heart and mind.

Your situation is unique. I don't know what specifically happened to you but I do know that God wants to show you His love, that He does care and that He's at work right now in your situation. It may take time for that truth to take root but keep believing and trusting God to make that truth a reality.

If you're not sure, pray right now and ask God to show you the truth about your heart toward Him. As David said, "Search me and know me" (Psalm 139). And he also said in Psalm 51, "Create in a me a clean heart, oh God, and renew a right spirit in me. Cast me not away from your presence oh Lord, and take not your Holy Spirit from me. Restore to me, the joy of my salvation. And renew a right spirit within me." Observe what pain has been holding you captive. Perhaps it's something that someone's done to you or something that has happened to you. Perhaps a tragedy, pain from health issues, or abuse. Whatever that thing is, God wants to reveal it to you so you can start healing from it. He has to remove the bullet in order to sew up the wound. Begin asking Him today the questions that are on your mind and listen to what He says—it may surprise you!

CHAPTER 2

Am I a 'Bad' Christian if I Struggle?

It's the question most of us will ask at some point or another, but we would not typically say out-loud. Struggle seems to be synonymously associated with lack of faith or lack of trust. Some even believe struggle is connected to sin—known or unknown—in someone's life for which God is purposely punishing them. But both of these assumptions are wrong. (I will show you why when we look at some Scripture later.)

Struggle is messy, like the outside of a syrup bottle that's been poured by sticky-fingered children and the calloused layers are built up into a crystallized goop that clogs the cap and runs down the side. Once you go to touch the bottle, the sticky sap works its way in-between the grooves of your fingerprints and you are now just as sticky as the sap you touched. It's messy and frustrating. You count in your mind how many times you've told the kids to wipe the bottle when it gets like that. You pickup a hot, soapy cloth and begin to let the warmth wipe away the layers of stickiness and goop, revealing the shiny surface underneath. Before long, the once-marred bottle that expelled its sticky sap on everything it touched, is now clean and pristine and ready to be a vessel for future use.

That's much like how the Holy Spirit works in our lives, taking the warm, soapy cloth and wiping away the layers of mess that mar us; restoring us. As we open ourselves to His hand of restoration and we trust in God to transform our minds and hearts, we are restored and ready for use again.

Struggle, like many things, is a messy word but it's also seen as as a negative thing in our society today. We will do almost anything to avoid being uncomfortable, or have any form of struggle in any way. We avoid it like the smelly dumpster on the other side of the street. We act like it's not a big deal on the surface but when confronted with the opportunity to go through struggle, we will fight, kick and scream to get away from it, running as if being chased by a thief, adrenaline pumping to bring us into safety. And who wouldn't want to avoid struggle? It's hard! It's ugly. It's often sad, discouraging and painful. It pushes you to limits you *didn't ever want to know you had*. It can be long and drawn out, or quick and extremely intense. It conjures up images like that of a hiker trying to reach the summit, dripping in sweat and toiling step by step to get to the very top, outstretching her trembling hand to reach the flag, inching closer with each push. Images like a family holding their beloved's hand as they struggle to say goodbye to their loved one who's battled cancer for the past four years. It can bring up memories of past traumas which once again resurface in the mind and bring forth emotions and tears. It is like an onion that keeps peeling back layer after layer, again and again, squeezing tears from your eyes with each layer shed. It's like an archaeologist who digs below the surface, unearthing a massive dinosaur, bone by bone with nothing but a tiny pickaxe and a dusting brush, pushing away the dirt, grain-of-sand by grain-of-sand.

But struggle also has another side, a hidden side that is often passed over and unseen. It's a side that is illusive and nearly invisible, only seen by the trained eye. If this hidden side was more popular, more clearly noticed, struggle would have a different association altogether. If we could dress it up in heels and slap a coat of lipstick on, it might look more appealing. It would be celebrated at the end, and even cherished in the middle of the struggle.

As Joyce Meyer says, "We live life forward but we often understand it backwards" (@JoyceMeyer). It usually takes coming out of the struggle to see this other side, but even then it is not always recognized. Many have become hard-hearted or the struggle has turned them a dark shade of grey. They have lost their footing in the climb and tumbled back down, broken and bruised without any desire to climb back up.

This other side of the struggle that I speak of; the product and the after-effects of struggle is *the growth in the struggle*. Now before you start throwing things at me, give me a moment to explain.

There are lessons that we can only learn in the midst of adversity. There is strength that is built inside of you when you struggle but persevere. There is endurance that is hard-wired inside of you which is suddenly birthed in the moments you propel forward in the face of defeat. The fortitude that gives you the strength to fight yet another day towards victory. *That* is the other side of struggle. It's not popular and you have to look for it, but it's there. Growth and fortitude are not built by being comfortable; character is not produced and expanded by staying still. Being strong and courageous, learning lessons and counting blessings is not often built on the back of comfort and leisure but rather on the other end of a messy but conquered battle.

I realize as I write this that to some it may seem I'm idealizing or simplifying struggle. To those of you who've endured great struggles, my words may seem empty. You may be thinking I haven't endured the sickening pain you have. You may have watched a child pass away, or been abused by someone in your family. You may have been living on the street or pushed into a life you didn't choose. You may have been betrayed by a spouse cheating or leaving you. There are so many tragic things that can happen in one's life. Maybe your tragedy is not as extreme as these but it is still painful. No amount of me saying "see the growth in the struggle" makes that pain dissipate. In fact, it may anger you to even hear me suggest that. I get it and I accept that. And you can know that God gets it even more than I do. Be honest with Him about your feelings; you don't need to sugar-coat them for Him. He already knows how you feel anyway:

> "You know when I sit and when I rise; you perceive my thoughts from afar. You discern my going out and my lying down; you are

familiar with all my ways. Before a word is on my tongue, you, Lord, know it completely" Psalm 139:2-4 (NIV).

I don't want to trivialize anyone's pain. Each person's story is unique. Some stories seem more painful than others, but *pain is universal.* We can all understand pain in varying degrees. If you've experienced a little pain or a lot, each wound needs to be brought before God and healed by His loving hand. You cannot ignore the pain or it will continue to fester. On the other side of the spectrum, don't feel you have to be tough and ignore the little pains you're feeling. God cares about the little and the big problems. He wants to heal you from them all, so you can begin moving forward in freedom and peace.

Battles and struggles are not easy or enjoyable. They often bring out a lot of things in us that are not desirable, but it says in Romans 5:3-5 that, "we can rejoice, too, when we run into problems and trials, for we know that they help us develop **endurance**. And **endurance** develops **strength of character**, and character strengthens our confident hope of salvation. And this hope will not lead to disappointment. For we know how dearly God loves us, because He has given us the Holy Spirit to fill our hearts with His love" (emphasis mine).

Reading this passage, you can see that God has given us the Holy Spirit to help us through these trials and struggles. We are not doing this alone or expected to figure it out by ourselves. We are not to be left to fend for ourselves, helpless and hopeless in this world. No! We are sons and daughters of Christ. He has bought us with a price and He has seated us in heavenly places, taking care of us and working good from our struggles:

> "And we know that God causes everything to work together for the good of those who love God and are called according to His purpose for them" Romans 8:28 (NLT).

No matter what troubles come our way, or what storms we face or the struggles that lie ahead, God is our guide and He will walk us through the storm.

And yet, even though all these things are true, it doesn't change the fact that struggle is still messy. The only thing that makes the mess bearable is the fact that Jesus is right there with us, in the storm and in the fire. He's holding our hand as we walk through the valley and He never lets go.

God Following His Plan, Not Ours

We see this demonstrated in the story of Shadrach, Meshach and Abednego. They were being persecuted for their faith for disregarding the law that they must bow down to the King of their land. They knew that the consequence was that they would be thrown in the fiery furnace, and perish. Even though I am sure they must have been afraid, it did not stop them from holding firm to their conviction, and the Bible says they had strong faith that God would save them. They were in the midst of a struggle and it may have looked to those around them like God had abandoned them. I believe that many must have pictured God handling it a different way. God rescuing us can look so different than what we imagine, yet we often expect it to happen a certain way. Had I been alive at that time, I would have expected God to strike the king dead, thus, saving Shad, Meesh, and Abed (as I like to call them) from death! Or, for the furnace to not light up, and a great rain to cover the land. In my humanness, I expect God to show up *before* the big disaster. In my humanness, I can mistakingly expect God to do things a certain way—my way. This perfectly exemplifies the limits of my human reasoning. I would never have imagined that instead, God would let them walk into the fiery furnace and save them from being burned!

As you can read in Daniel 3:16-28, Shad, Meesh, and Abed were facing walking into the furnace, which I'm sure they must have assumed meant sudden death. The king turned up the furnace to seven times its usual heat…talk about someone trying to make a statement! As they walked into the fire, I can only imagine they must have wondered if this was the end. I probably would have questioned whether God was going to save me at that point! Like I said, it's not how I would have imagined my rescue to play out. But just like a good storybook ending, instead of being consumed and murdered by the fire, God took them *through* the fire and they walked out of the furnace, without even the smell of smoke on them! Talk about a huge miracle; but even more than the miracle of being saved from death, is the miracle of their faith in God to save them. I would love to believe that I would have faith that God could still save me, even as I walked into the furnace, but I don't know if I would have. That takes big faith!

I think this is what we often do: we assume we know how God should rescue us from our struggles. We give Him a well-laid out, step-by-step rescue plan and expect Him to follow it. We think we know all the ins and outs of our situation. We are impatient in waiting to see what God does, and we keep asking for our will instead of God's. We may even lose faith that God is working in our situation because it hasn't happened the way we expected. We may be well-intentioned, but we are essentially telling God we don't trust Him; and in trying to do things in our own strength or our own way, we may miss out on the better plan that God has. But in this story, because of the demonstration of their faith, and there being *no* doubt that God had saved them, the king repented and decreed that everyone must serve the Lord! Isn't that just how God is? He takes a terrible situation and works good out of it!

> We give Him a well laid-out, step-by-step rescue plan and expect Him to follow it.

It's recorded in Daniel 3:24-25 that when the guards and the King looked inside to see if the men were in there, they saw a fourth man in there with them—Jesus! I think that's such an important point to notice: Jesus never leaves us in our struggles. He was right there with the three men, in the middle of the fire, to help guide them and walk them through. We may not see Him, we may not know He's there, but we can trust that He is with us. He is protecting us (Psalm 91), guiding us (Proverbs 16:9) and working it out for our good (Romans 8:28). Look up these verses and study them. Let them remind you of the truth.

We don't hear any more about these brave men after this record of them but I've often wondered what their lives were like after that. I can only imagine that they were forever changed. Did they go on to lead normal lives? Did they get married? Did they sit down by the warm fire with their young, freckle-faced toddlers and tell them the story of the time they were saved from the fiery furnace? I can only surmise because we don't hear more about them after that experience (other than that they were promoted to a high position) but I cannot imagine how you could go through an experience like that and not be changed.

Isn't that the beauty of what God does? He takes us through the fire, walks alongside us so we are not alone, and then changes our lives by *changing us* through the experience. What are you facing that's hard right now? What are you hoping and trusting in God for? Do you believe He will answer your cry? The struggle, or the fire, is not fun. It's often hard and can be scary to face, but as we trust in God and rely on His hand to guide us, we are changed and transformed from the inside, out. What does that mean? It means that He does a work in us that we cannot see, but little by little, He recreates our nature and builds us up inside until the character that He's building shows up in our actions and our thoughts. "Therefore we do not lose heart. Though outwardly we are wasting away, yet **inwardly we are being renewed day by day**" 2 Corinthians 14:6 (NIV, emphasis mine).

Our character, our faith, our spiritual maturity is like a seed that's been planted in the ground. It starts off small, but as it's given what it needs such as sunlight, water and nutrients, it begins to sprout roots, and then stems and leaves; before long, the little seed has become a beautiful plant. Much in the same way, as we are given what we need by God (the Word, spending time with Him, listening for His voice, sometimes even trials that teach us things), we grow in Him and His nature grows in us.

In John 15, it talks about how God is the Vine and we are the branches and when we abide in Him, He abides in us. We cannot do it on our own; we need God as the vine to make us strong and grow His nature inside of us. Doing it alone in certain instances may seem possible, but we are only spiritually strong when we partner with God. His plans are only good— He can see all the moving parts—but our understanding is limited. Anyone may do life alone, but we have the gift of being led by the Holy Spirit: to learn from Him, to see things through God's eyes and to be part of the Vine that is life-giving to us (the branches).

Believing the Lie that Struggle Equals Lack of Faith and/or Sin

As I have already mentioned, there is a lie out there that says if you have struggles, you must be lacking faith, or that you must have sinned and the trial you are facing is God's way of punishing you. That lie is straight from the pit of hell. We live under the new covenant of grace and although our wrong decisions can lead to consequences, God is not raining down judgement on His people in the form of punishments.

In John 9, Jesus and His disciples encounter a man who had been blind from birth. The disciples ask Jesus, "Who sinned, this man or His parents, that He should be born blind?"

"'Neither this man nor His parents sinned,' said Jesus, 'but this happened so that the works of God might be displayed in Him'" (John 9:2-3, NIV).

"For God did not send His Son into the world to condemn the world, but to save the world through Him" John 3:17 (NIV).

We need to stop judging ourselves and others for the struggles we see in their lives and assuming that we know anything about 'why.' Some things are just going to be mysteries to which only God knows the answers. I, like many others, have asked the question as to why unspeakable tragedies happen. I have wondered why some mothers lose their children to car accidents or cancer, why floods wipe out cities, and so many other things. I will likely never know the reasons why, and God doesn't owe me the answers either. Faith is trusting in God even when you *don't* have the answers; in fact, I would go so far as to say faith is trusting God *in spite* of not having answers and not even needing to know the answers.

I was praying one day, and God said to me, "Struggle in life does not mean failure in faith." Immediately, it repaired something in my heart. It repaired a hole in my heart that I didn't realize I had gaping open. I realized I had believed the opposite. It was something I had always sort of believed in the back of my head but had never really given it the words or thought about it a lot. I had believed the lie that if I struggled or went through trials in life, it must be because I didn't do things right or that I lacked faith. But when God spoke that truth to me, immediately I realized that I had believed the lie that some of the struggles I had faced in my life were a result of lack of faith, or a result of some unknown sin, but that's not the way God works. I had believed that if I'd only had more faith, I would have overcome or I would have avoided that storm. I also realized it was a lie of the enemy that I had believed, and I repented immediately. I thanked God for revealing this to me and I was so overjoyed for His perfect truth to set me free. I see that promise reflected in Scripture:

"For by grace you have been saved through faith. And this is not your own doing; it is the gift of God" Ephesians 2:8 (NIV).

"Therefore, since we have been justified by faith, we have peace with God through our Lord Jesus Christ" Romans 5:1 (NIV).

See, I think as humans we often associate struggle with failure, or we associate struggle with lack of faith. Even though we know that we will have trouble in this life—it says so right in Scripture—we somehow think that we can avoid it with enough faith. However, Jesus was clear:

"I have told you these things, so that in me you may have peace. In this world you will have trouble. But take heart! I have overcome the world" John 16:33 (NIV).

If you follow the logic that we can avoid struggle with enough faith, it means that the mother whose child is riddled with cancer would be guilty of lack of faith for her child to be healed. Or that the child is not healed because of his/her own lack of faith. Or it would mean that the person who got in a terrible car wreck was being punished by God for their sin. That's a huge lie because as it says in the verse above, and in Ephesians 2:8, we have been saved by grace! Can you imagine a God who would punish His people, who He lovingly creates and promises to take care of all the days of their lives, because they lack faith? That is the exact opposite of everything we know to be true about God. It's the opposite of all the stories we read throughout the Bible when even though God's people sinned, He continued to forgive them over and over again and give them chance after chance. When He was ready to deal with them harshly, He instead had compassion and mercy for them. Over and over again we see the character of God as a loving, gracious, merciful and overwhelmingly compassionate Father. All throughout Scripture, we learn of God's character with these attributes.

Yet, sadly, this is the lie that enemy has tried to trick people into believing, Christians and unbelievers alike. The lie that we struggle because we just don't have enough faith, or that God is punishing us. It's hard to imagine that anyone would believe this lie if they love God and know He loves them, yet it's a lie that the enemy has snuck into our minds, like a child who quickly places a candy bar on the checkout belt when her mom is about to pay. It's quick and it often goes unnoticed and unchecked.

We need to remember that even though this is a lie, we don't have to believe it and the Word of God shows us the truth. Really meditate on the scriptures below and see the truth that God is a loving and compassionate God. Yes, He does correct us (Proverbs 3:12: "For whom the Lord loves He reproves, Even as a father corrects the son in whom He delights") but His correction is always done in kindness and for our good. It is correction, not condemnation.

"How abundant are the good things that you have stored up for those who fear you, that you bestow in the sight of all, on those who take refuge in you. In the shelter of your presence you hide them from all human intrigues" Psalm 31:19-20 (NIV).

"The Lord is good to all; He has compassion on all He has made" Psalm 145:9 (NIV).

In Matthew 7:11 it says, "If you then, being evil, know how to give good gifts to your children, how much more will your Father who is in heaven give good things to those who ask Him!" This verse makes a good point. To those reading this who are parents, there is no denying you would do anything that is good for your kids. You would never be evil towards them. You would not deny them the good things in life, or deny fulfilling their needs, even if what they wanted seemed good to them. You wouldn't let them have it because you knew it could bring harm.

For example, it may look 'good' to your child for you to buy them every toy they ever wanted but as their parent, you know that's not *good* for them. Your discipline implementing healthy boundaries may be perceived by the child as unfair, but you are doing it for his or her own good. Or, if your son or daughter were in danger, you would do anything within your power to help them or remove the danger, even putting your own life in danger.

We are limited in our ability as humans to love our children as completely, perfectly and unconditionally as our Father in heaven. Yet, even we would do those things for our children. As this verse points out, if we only want good things for our children, how much more does God want to give us good things? He knows what is best for us, and He sees the whole picture (which we never can) and because of that, we should be content to know that in God's goodness, He would never purpose for anything bad to happen to us. Yes, bad things do happen, but that does not mean God is doing those things, or punishing us. He wants only good for His children. We need to know the truth that God cares for us, loves us and has good plans for our lives (Jeremiah 29:11). We can trust and believe that truth, or we can go on believing the lie of the enemy that our lack of faith or our sin is what's causing struggle in our lives. The problem with the latter is that we not only believe a lie, but we now put immense pressure on ourselves to be perfect in order to counteract any more sin resulting in punishment. That's called 'working for your salvation' and it goes against Scripture in which salvation is a free gift, bought by Jesus' sacrifice on the cross.

> "For I know the plans I have for you," declares the Lord, "plans to prosper you and not to harm you, plans to give you hope and a future" Jeremiah 29:11 (NIV).

Then Why Doesn't God Step in Immediately?

There are no answers for this question, as well as many answers for this question, none of which I would surmise or be prideful enough to say I have all the answers. God has His reasons. He is Sovereign, and His ways are higher than mine, and I cannot start to question His will or His ways. I cannot understand all the struggles in the world and account for why each one happens. I cannot fathom all the reasons why, or begin to think I deserve to know. That's part of the reasoning trap that we are prone to get into that I will talk about later as it's a dangerous one. I have learned to trust His timing, will and ways as I've walked with Him. It doesn't mean it isn't still hard at times not to ask the *'why'* questions but it's a choice I've had to make. My experience with God is that He is true, always faithful, gracious, merciful and compassionate, and He always has good plans for me. The beautiful truth is that not only have I experienced all of those things, but I can back all of those promises up with Scripture. With that winning combination, the *'why'* doesn't matter as much.

But, having said that, I believe that sometimes one of the reasons that the struggles are not as quickly resolved as we'd like is that God wants us to grow in Him as we wait for His rescue. We also cannot discount that God *is* at work in our situations, even if we can't see or feel it. He is always at work. He does not rest, so we can be assured that even if we don't see the answer to our prayers immediately, He is still at work in it. "But Jesus replied, 'My Father is always working, and so am I'" John 5:17 (NLT).

> "So let's not get tired of doing what is good. At just the right time we will reap a harvest of blessing if we don't give up" Galatians 6:9 (NLT).

He wants us to *see* firsthand His faithfulness in walking us through the storm. He wants you to know the sound of His voice as He directs you down the path that will lead you to freedom. Spiritually, He wants you to feel His heart beating as you seek refuge in His arms. He wants you to know, intimately, the goodness and breadth of His love that surpasses all understanding and knowledge. He desires for you to see the beauty of abiding in Him as you take each day, step by step. He longs for you to learn to trust in Him for your victory. And that means that you have to have something to trust in Him for.

The easy path doesn't require trust or faith. It's easy, but it doesn't grow you at all. Think about it like a tour guide that's been assigned to you for the day. You have two journeys to make, neither of which do you know where you're going. The tour guide can only guide you on one of your two journeys. One is to the grocery store, one block away. The store is a short walk, the sidewalk has no turns or bends in it and you know you simply have to walk in a straight line and you will arrive at your destination. The other path is at the top of a steep mountain. It requires a combination of multiple paths that connect, as well as steep inclines and knowing which direction you're going as there are no signs. Which journey would you rather have your tour guide leading you on? The easy path doesn't require much of anyone. It's simple, straightforward and no special requirements are needed of you. The mountainous climb, however, will be harder, but you will gain a greater sense of accomplishment, build some muscle and stamina along the way, as well as see the view at the end that will far surpass the easy block to the grocery store.

Likewise, life's hard path will have struggles along the way, and it requires a faith and trust that's grown through adversity. But when you reach the other side of victory and triumph, you can look back and see God's hand directing and guiding your steps as well as His footsteps alongside yours, each step of the way. You can feel the sense of accomplishment in your adversity and the view is a thousand times better when you reach the other side. That is what bonds your heart and mind in Christ (see Philippians 4:7), your tour guide in life. That is what allows you to *know* Him (not just read about Him) as your Friend, your Protector and your Faithful Victor. And that, my friend, is worth a *million* easy paths.

Firsthand Experience

Seeing, experiencing and walking the journey firsthand is much different than someone else telling you about it. For example, have you ever had a friend tell you about a really exciting experience? Perhaps they travelled to a new country: As they tell you about their experience, although you're excited for them, it's not the same experience for you as it was for them. You have to imagine in your mind what they're telling you. You have to get creative and ask questions to help you understand. They've got all the smells, sounds and sights from their experience locked up in their minds but you can only experience it by what they share and you must use your imagination to try to picture what they're describing. They are forever tied to those experiences in their heart. You can experience their excitement, but it's not the same as you experiencing it yourself.

Much in the same way, hearing someone tell you about the goodness of God is much different than experiencing it yourself. Hearing someone tell you that God is faithful is much different than spending 40 years seeing and experiencing the faithfulness of God for yourself. Listening to someone explain the closeness of God being as near as their own breath while they were in the midst of a storm is encouraging, but differs from you having experienced that same nearness yourself. *We cannot tattoo ourselves with others' experiences of God.* A tattoo resembles an image, but it is merely that—an illusion. It sits on the surface and cannot penetrate inside. It's like trying to make the glass slipper fit the step-sister, Drizella.

It won't happen. Its curvatures and design was made only to fit Cinderella and no amount of shoving, shaping and squishing will make Drizella's foot fit.

God has His own personal relationship with each of us and we cannot expect to experience it through osmosis from those around us. That doesn't mean that we necessarily want to go through trials. I don't think anyone would want to willingly do that, but at the same time, God will not allow more to come on us than we can bear (see below) and if we can trust in Him to bring us through the storm, we will be more intertwined with Him and His heart than we were before the storm. We will be that much more embedded in Him and that much more of His character will be embedded in us, and working inside us and flowing out of us. No, it's not easy. I will never expect you to believe that. But I will tell you that if you can hold on with faith, trust in God to deliver you and give your heart to Him to hold through it all, He will walk you through the storm, and bring you safely to the other side.

We cannot tattoo ourselves with others' experiences of God.

> "No temptation has overtaken you except what is common to mankind. And God is faithful; He will not let you be tempted beyond what you can bear. But when you are tempted, He will also provide a way out so that you can endure it" 1 Corinthians 10:13 (NIV).

CHAPTER 3

The Root of Bitterness

A common temptation when we are facing struggles is to allow bitterness to take root when we are in the midst of the storm. The problem with bitterness is that it's sneaky. It masquerades as human nature, so no one notices it come in the back door. It's like a prowler surveilling a house, planning his route of attack and learning the rhythms and schedules of those who live there. He waits until he has learned all he can know about the occupants and then, when they are unaware, away or asleep, he slyly sneaks in the back widow, without making so much as a peep. Before anyone is aware of what's going on, he's already made his move and taken anything of value. He knows just how much time it will take and plans how far away he will be when the occupants discover this infiltration has occurred.

Bitterness is much the same. It doesn't parade itself around and walk through the front door. It's much more comfortable slipping in quietly through the back door. It's a tool that the enemy uses to plan his attack. It's coordinated right down to the last detail. It's sneaky, just like the prowler. Once bitterness is inside, the damage it does is immense. It steals joy and peace, it steals love and it steals anything of value. It has no shame destroying as much as it can in as little time as possible.

However, just as homeowner's insurance will cover the cost of replacing those stolen items, Jesus comes in and restores the things that were stolen from us, two-fold, when we repent and turn our eyes towards Him.

> "Instead of your shame you will receive a double portion, and instead of disgrace you will rejoice in your inheritance. And so you will inherit a **double portion** in your land, and everlasting joy will be yours" Isaiah 61:7 (NIV, emphasis mine).

Why are we discussing bitterness? Bitterness is a big part of the picture when it comes to dealing with struggles. Not everyone who goes through a difficult season will be bitter. Some people handle it with such grace and endurance that it amazes me. But for a large majority of people, bitterness begins to eat away at them, even unknowingly. Although it's a sneaky guest when it arrives, as it settles in it's easy to recognize the signs:
- you're angry when good things happen to others
- you feel like you're the only one who's been dealt a bad hand
- you compare yourself or your situations to others
- you're jealous
- you have a negative outlook and attitude on life
- you expect the worst to happen

- you feel as if no one understands your struggles, even God

It may be some of these or all of these.

Bitterness is a lonely place to be. It comes with a lot of shame and guilt. And because it's sneaky, it takes up residence before you've been able to recognize what it's doing to you. It steals your joy and peace. It robs you of being happy when good things happen to others. It makes you negative and lacking in compassion. But more than all of that, it alters your view of God. It changes you into someone who doesn't understand the God who created you. It leads you to question God's goodness, His character, His hand in your life and for some, His very existence.

So why do we become bitter? In the midst of terrible circumstances, why is it so hard to hold onto faith for better days? Why do we struggle to believe the promises in Jeremiah 29:11 that God has good plans for us and instead, we believe we are destined to heartache like Job? Why do we begin to believe the lie that we are the only ones facing struggle when we are in the middle of it?

Simply put, it's because we don't do 'struggle' very well. Our emotions get in the way and we want to have someone to blame. The enemy knows that and he tries to manipulate the truth into a lie, to try to make you believe that God has left you, just like the Israelites believed when they were wandering in the desert.

It's the oldest story in the book: Adam and Eve. Satan tempted Eve to believe that God didn't want her to have the fruit because then she would be like God. He planted doubt in her mind. She believed him, despite what God had told her. The enemy knows that if he can whisper even a doubt that God isn't fully good, he can start to work at making you believe that God will not deliver you.

Eve was not out looking to be deceived or to question God. Yet the enemy told just enough of a lie to place doubt in her mind. He twisted the truth just enough to cause her to question.

The enemy knows that if he makes up a blatantly obvious lie, it won't be convincing. But if he can make up enough of a lie to sound true, or have the ring of truth, there's a chance you'll believe it. And on top of that, he waits for an opportune time to strike. In the middle of a struggle or trial, is often when you're the most weak, the most vulnerable and less likely to be on guard against the enemy's attacks.

> "When the devil had finished tempting Jesus, He left Him until the next opportunity came" Luke 4:13 (NLT).

Think about when you're sick, physically, like when you have the flu. If you're in the middle of the sickness, and you're feverish, tired, congested and feeling terrible, you're much less able to accomplish anything. Something as simple as heating up a pot of soup is an immense task, and you need a few hours just to recover from that small output of work. You may need someone you love to come alongside you and nourish you back to health. They may cook or clean for you, or be there to help you in any way you need it.

In the same way, when you're going through a difficult season — a trial, a struggle—you're more vulnerable to the enemy's attacks because your energy is going into overcoming the trial. Your energy is often directed at having the strength to endure with God's help. You are focused on pushing forward and getting through. Your focus isn't often on what lies the enemy is feeding you and as such, your guard is down.

I have faced many struggles, as most have. Some have been minor but hard nonetheless, and others have taken me a longer time to recover from. As with varying degrees of physical illness, there are varying degrees of struggle. In the times when I have faced mountainous giants, I rely on God as my air, my breath, my every waking moment. Just like it says in James 4:8, *He draws near to me as I draw near to Him* and in those times, I can feel Him closer to me than my own breath. He hems me in, underneath the shadow of His wing (Psalm 91:1) and He weathers the storm with me. His grace is *sufficient* for me and His power is made perfect in *my weakness* (2 Corinthians 12:9). It's one of those truths that we don't perhaps realize is there until we need it. All of the sudden you realize its importance. It's still hard, but I know that I can make it through with *Christ who is my strength* (Philippians 4:13). Without Him, I am nothing and I know that I need to rely on Him daily, moment by moment sometimes, to have the strength to make it through. In those hardest of moments, I am focused on my Redeemer, not my opponent.

Yet, as it says in 1 Peter 5:8, we need to be ever watchful of the enemy: "Stay alert! Watch out for your great enemy, the devil. He prowls around like a roaring lion, looking for someone to devour. Stand firm against him, and be strong in your faith. Remember that your family of believers all over the world is going through the same kind of suffering you are" (NLT). That is where prayer comes in as well as putting on the armour of God, and waiting on the Lord to fight your battles for you.

> "This is what the LORD says to you: 'Do not be afraid or discouraged because of this vast army. For the battle is not yours, but God's" 2 Chronicles 20:15 (NIV).

You cannot rely on your own strength to fight the enemy; you will become drained when you're working from your own strength, which is limited. Instead we need to call upon the Lord, knowing He will hide us under the shadow of His wing, and we wait for Him go to battle for us—working from His Sovereign power that never runs out.

It is when I am in those intense struggles that the enemy will try to sneak in thoughts causing bitterness and anger, resentment and discouragement. It took me going through a number of struggles (and the discernment of the Holy Spirit) before I realized the patterns of the enemy's plots. With the leadership of the Holy Spirit, keeping me watchful for lies, I was able to instead seek the Lord for the truth. It caused me to turn to the Word of God instead of believing whatever lie the enemy would have me believe. I would love to say that I have never believed a single lie of the enemy but that is simply not true. Until I had really surrendered my mind to Christ, I was believing many lies of the enemy. It wasn't until I started recognizing the lies and studying the Word that I started to gain 'faith muscles' in knowing the truth and believing that I would see it at work in my life.

Where has Bitterness Taken Root in You?

Being bitter toward God makes you bitter toward others, circumstances or relationships. It can make you bitter or resentful of the good things that happen to those around you. It steals joy from your life. Bitterness breeds more bitterness and it begins to take root in new areas and in new ways. It's poisonous to you and your relationship with God and people, even though you may not be aware that you're bitter. It is sneaky because it can start to warp your thinking and you may not even know it.

I can think of a specific experience where I noticed this in my own life. It's embarrassing to even admit, but by being transparent with you, I feel led to share raw and real experiences from my own life that have taught me. These personal and vulnerable experiences that I share from my life also show God's ability to highlight our wrong thinking and they are a testimony to that. And if I know one thing, it's that testimony breeds more testimony, more faith and hope. Let me share my story with you.

I specifically remember the day. It had been a particularly hard one and by the end of it, I was exhausted. I was in the middle of my own intense struggle and I was so fatigued. Physically, mentally and emotionally. I was ready for bed.

I got a text from a friend. She had been struggling with some physical pain, and she had asked me to pray for her. This is not an uncommon occurrence for me. I am often asked to pray for friends and I love being able to intercede for them. But this time was different. As she was telling me about her issue, inside of me rose up a bitter attitude, in that I felt like she had nothing to complain about because my struggle at the time, I felt, was much greater than hers. I had been struggling with this issue for over two years and here she had been struggling with it for a mere three days and she was ready to give up, completely frustrated. I began to feel frustration about her request rising up in my mind, out of nowhere. I mean, this was a surprise to me at the time because I truly love this person, and I have only ever wanted the best for her. We have shared many years together and in my wildest dreams I would never have imagined I could react in such a heartless and bitter way. I was honestly shocked with myself! I felt the Holy Spirit speak up and say, "Stop." I paused for a moment, and realized the past few thoughts that had trickled through my mind. At the moment that I recognized it, I immediately repented and I was really surprised (not in a good way) at the bitter attitude that had sneakily risen up in me. I was so embarrassed and disappointed in myself but I also knew there had to be a reason behind it. This was not like me at all.

But as I began to pray about it and ask God to show me where that bitterness came from, the Holy Spirit began to speak to me about the journey through pain that I was on, and how when we go through struggles and pain, how important it is to keep our hearts postured towards Him. What I mean by that is we have to be so diligent in recognizing our thoughts, our mindsets and our pattern of reasoning. What had seemed like an 'out of nowhere' response for me, was actually a pattern of negative thinking, over a period of time. It was months of me unknowingly feeling that what was happening to me was unfair. It was months of me feeling sorry for myself. It was months of me looking only at myself, my pain, my struggle and not looking at Jesus and what *He* was doing in the situation.

I tell you that vulnerable and raw story to demonstrate that:

a) You're not alone. We all get off track in our thinking at times but we can always trust the Holy Spirit to show us when we need to pivot.

And…

b) Even though that was a hard reality to face, it was also a moment of reckoning. A moment where I could repent of my behaviour, turn away from it and let God come in and start revealing the *truth* to me. In doing so, it set me free from holding onto the bitterness in my heart that I didn't realize was there. See how sneaky it can be?

The truth is that my heart of empathy is always seeking and asking God to show me who I can help. In my prayers, my contention is to continually ask God to show me who is in need, who I can help and who I can pray for. That's the truth. That's what rooted down deep on the inside of me. That's my spirit and my soul calling out to God and it's the cry of my heart. This bitterness was something that I had unknowingly let in and it took the Holy Spirit awakening me to this realization.

My empathetic and compassionate heart often breaks for those around me. It used to really weigh on me because I felt helpless to do anything to help them. But as I've grown up in the Lord, He's shown me that He's given me that heart so that I can intercede for others. I find that when I'm given the opportunity to pray for others, my broken heart immediately heals because I know that instead of being helpless to aid that person, I can give them and their situation to God, who has the most capable hands possible. He can do in one second what I could not do, even in 100 years.

But in that moment when the Holy Spirit revealed that bitterness in me, I was thankful that He showed me so that I could pray about it and let God heal that bitterness, which was unrelated to the person, but instead something I was wrestling with inside myself. It allowed me to take time over the next few weeks to really seek the Lord and ask Him to change my heart of bitterness, change my heart of feeling sorry for myself and instead really *actively* begin looking around at all that God *was* doing in my situation and how He wanted me to pray for those around me.

> "For the LORD corrects those He loves, just as a father corrects a child in whom He delights" Proverbs 3:12 (NLT).

> "For the LORD disciplines those He loves, and He punishes each one He accepts as His child" Hebrews 12:6 (NLT).

That's why this verse has always been a huge comfort to me. I do not despise the chastisement or correction of the Lord because I know it means He's changing me and creating new thinking in me! He wants to take me out of my wrong thinking and wrong or damaging patterns and place my thinking and my feet on a rock of hope and truth!

Now that we've talked about how sneaky bitterness is, how it alters our thinking, and the signs of bitterness, you may be asking how to overcome it.

First of all, the fact that you're recognizing it and want to change shows that the Holy Spirit is speaking to you too, and will be alongside to help guide you to right thinking.

It's actually very simple and not at all complicated. It comes down to two things: prayer and the Word. I would say that those two things things are the solution to 100% of our problems. Prayer is powerful and we know that God goes to work on our requests, when we ask His will. His will is to uproot bitterness (Ephesians 4:31) and to create in us a clean heart. So you can be assured that when you ask for these good things, God is already there, answering your prayer.

Be patient with yourself; it doesn't happen overnight. If it's been a long time of bitterness taking root in you, much like pulling a large weed, it will take more time and effort to pull out than a tiny weed. Give God the time and have patience to let Him do a new work inside of you. "For I am about to do something new. See, I have already begun! Do you not see it? I will make a pathway through the wilderness. I will create rivers in the dry wasteland" (Isaiah 43:19 NLT).

Pray about your struggle—daily—as many times as you're aware of it or tempted to worry. As it says in 1 Thessalonians 5:16, *pray continuously*, without ceasing. (It also says in that verse to *rejoice* and *give thanks*! Let that also be a part of your daily prayers!) Then let God do the work that only He can do. You *will* begin to see a change!

The other part is to begin studying the Word in the area of bitterness, and see what God says about it. Here are a few scriptures to get you started:

> "Strive for peace with everyone, and for the holiness without which no one will see the Lord. See to it that no one fails to obtain the grace of God; that no "root of bitterness" springs up and causes trouble, and by it many become defiled" Hebrews 12:14-15 (ESV).

> "Be kind to one another, tenderhearted, forgiving one another, as God in Christ forgave you." Ephesians 4:32 (ESV).

> "I have said these things to you, that in me you may have peace. In the world you will have tribulation. But take heart; I have overcome the world" John 16:33 (ESV).

> "Lo, for my own welfare I had great bitterness; It is You who has kept my soul from the pit of nothingness, for You have cast all my sins behind Your back" Isaiah 38:17 (NASB).

> "Create in me a pure heart, O God, and renew a steadfast spirit within me" Psalm 51:10 (NIV).

There are many more passages of Scripture on this and I really encourage you to take the time to look into the scriptures about getting rid of bitterness, and study about kindness and joy, which is the opposite of bitterness. Taking time to pray and study the Word is the 'prescription' for the issue of bitterness. It says in James 1:5 that, "if any of you lacks wisdom, you should ask God, who gives generously to all without finding fault, and it will be given to you"(NIV). He will give you wisdom to change your thinking. He will transform your mind and give you the ability to overcome, *without finding fault*! **That is the God we serve!** Even in His correction, He shows us how much He cares about us, and for us. He doesn't want us living in negative thinking because that leads to a sad and miserable life. He wants to highlight our wrong thinking and give us the wisdom and ability to change it to right thinking! That is a loving and caring God!

Take this verse as an encouragement to keep going! God is building good character in you through your struggles:

> "Consider it pure joy, my brothers and sisters, whenever you face trials of many kinds, because you know that the testing of your faith produces perseverance. Let perseverance finish its work so that you may be mature and complete, not lacking anything" James 1:2-4 (NIV).

> "And we boast in the hope of the glory of God. Not only so, but we also glory in our sufferings, because we know that suffering

produces perseverance; perseverance, character; and character, hope" Romans 5:2-4 (NIV).

Know that God is at Work!

When you go through struggle, it's so easy to look at what *isn't* happening rather than what is. It takes effort to look at what God is doing. It takes courage to read the Word and believe the promises God has given us in there while you're still in the middle of the struggle. It takes determination and a soft heart to trust the promises of God instead of trusting how we feel.

It's like when you accidentally cut your finger while cooking (this has happened to me too many times to count). You bandage the wound and you trust in the fact that it will clot and that over time it will heal. You cannot measure the healing or watch it happen moment by moment. You could stare at the cut all day long and you wouldn't be able to watch it heal. But as time goes on, it indeed begins to heal and soon enough the bandaid comes off and the cut seals itself off. Then you notice it scabs. And before long, the scab falls off and reveals fresh and new skin. This takes a few days and yet if you were to stare incessantly at your finger for those few days, you would not be able to 'see' it heal. In the same way, we cannot always see what God is doing. He is at work in our situation, just like He's at work healing the cut, but if we try to watch Him in action we can't always see it. We have to trust that He is at work because He *says* He is. When Jesus was working on the Sabbath, the Pharisees tried to persecute Him but He reminded them: "'My

Father is working until now, and I Myself am working'" John 5:17 (NIV).

He is *always, always, always* working! We can be assured that He's not sleeping on the job or that He will 'get to it later.' No, He is at work right now, even when we can't see it. That is part of what builds our faith. If we could always see the way He was orchestrating things we would have no need for faith or trust. It is when we rely on Him *without* knowing, that our faith grows. That's why God reminds me often that my victory is not dependent on my understanding. If I rely on myself to understand what God's doing, I will most likely get frustrated, or I won't be putting my faith and hope in Him. I'll be putting my faith in myself and, let's be honest, I'm not all that capable. But God is, and He wants you to trust in Him that even though you can't see what He's doing, He's at work on your situation.

To be fair, there are times when God reveals the work He's doing. He will give me a verse as an encouragement or perhaps speak through a friend, and I treasure those moments. It spurs on my hope and encourages me to keep my faith stirred up. Especially when you're first learning to rely on God and stop meddling all the time, He will show up in noticeable ways and give you confirmations and encouragements to show Himself faithful. He wants you to be confident in Him. He wants to show you that you can trust and rely on Him by giving you affirmations along the way. As you grow in your faith, perhaps there won't be as many confirmations because you've learned to rely on Him without as much hand-holding, but that doesn't mean He is any less at work than when He does give you affirmations. If we could get past our pre-conceived ideas of what God is doing and how He's doing it, we would be a lot more content. If we were able to just stop trying to ask God to do it a certain way and instead just pray for His will —in whichever way He chooses to go about it—we would be so much more at peace. There is a moment in everyone's walk when one has to make the decision to trust God and not oneself. Perhaps that's a daily decision for some of you; rarely is it a one-time commitment. Let go of the reigns and give Him that last ounce of control you've been trying to keep.

CHAPTER 4

Leave Reasoning Behind

One of the greatest moments of letting go of myself and trusting in God was when I let go of reasoning. God had been speaking to me for years about fully trusting in Him and although I wanted to, I also felt like I didn't know the practical steps in how to accomplish that. My heart was sold on the idea but my head was stuck. Have you ever felt that strange dichotomy?

That's when one day, the Holy Spirit said something so profound to me that it changed my entire outlook on how to trust God and how to move forward in peace. He said, "Your victory is not dependent on your understanding."

It took me a minute to digest the breadth of what He said. I was so concerned about 'figuring things out' all the time that in doing so, I had lost the childlike faith in trusting in God to know the answers. I had become completely self-reliant, which was really a form of arrogance. Because I had gone through so many struggles in my life, I had begun to feel like I needed to take care of myself. The message out in the world today is that you need to look out for yourself—number one. You need to be strong and independent—

take matters into your own hands. I began to feel like perhaps I needed to do the same. I began feeling like I needed to take control of things, that I had to direct the narrative of situations in my life, even though I didn't realize I had begun to think this way. Like *so many* things in life, because I wasn't remaining aware of my thoughts and guarding against the lies of the enemy, it just kind of snuck in—this sense of taking care of myself. I thought I felt empowered, but really, I felt immense pressure to get it right. Had I really stopped to assess the situation, I would have seen that it was God who was leading me on my path, and not myself at all. In my arrogance, I thought I had helped find solutions to my problems and in doing so, I had not given God the glory He deserved, and still deserves.

See, my struggles not only involved myself, but one of my most significant and hardest journeys involved my daughter. Out of respect for her, I won't share all of the details, but we embarked on a six year journey of figuring out a devastating diagnosis of a serious bone disease (similar to brittle bones), and our lives were changed in a moment. When the doctor tells you they'll do a test to rule out something worrisome, and then that test comes back positive, it's devastating.

It began when she turned one. She was a beautiful and vibrant little girl. She met all of her milestones early and surprised us all with how eloquently she spoke at such a young age. At 12 months old she was already putting two words together. We had no concerns about her development. But then something changed. One day, her two bottom baby teeth fell out. They initially grew in around 10 months and then at 12 months, they got loose one day and just fell out. No warning. I took her to the dentist and the doctor. They assured me that she must have just accidentally knocked them one day and that was what caused them to fall out. I wasn't buying it but there were no other plausible reasons they could provide so we left it at that.

A few months later, her top two front teeth came in. Then one by one, just like last time, they fell out. It was at this point that my concerns grew. I took her to our doctor and then a specialist. They couldn't find any reason for it and told me there was no reason to be concerned. It was just fluke. But it didn't stop there.

Then as she grew older, she wasn't progressing in walking. She was 15 months old and still crawling. I took her back to the doctor but they told me she was 'within normal range.' I continued to hear those words from every doctor and specialist I visited for the next 3 years. I began to despise that phrase. It grated on my heart because it meant there was nothing further to investigate and that I needed to let it go, yet a mother knows when something is wrong with her child. I spent a lot of time going between praying and crying, knowing in my heart that something was wrong, but no answers were ever laid at my feet.

I was determined to have answers, but everywhere I turned doors kept closing. Finally, I went to see my cousin, who happened to also be our local paediatrician. I explained that I felt something wasn't right but I needed her help as all the other doors were closed and it felt like none of the doctors believed me. It wasn't typical for a toddler's teeth to fall out for no reason. She had already lost five teeth by the age of three, yet somehow, none of the doctors I spoke with had any reason for concern. My cousin agreed to help and she began a series of tests. She wanted to start with a blood test to rule out an extremely rare bone disease.

One week later she called to give me the results. I didn't really give it much thought that week, assuming it would come back negative. But it didn't. Over the phone as she began to tell me the news, I sank. My heart sank. My feet felt like they were going to fall out from under me. I sat down at my kitchen table, listening to what she was saying but a thousand thoughts were pulsing through my mind: "*What would her future look like? This wasn't in our plan. Will she be okay? Is there treatment? Oh that's a good question,*" I thought.

"Okay. But, wait. Is there treatment?" I asked coyly, worried that since she hadn't offered any, the answer might be no.

"I'm sorry. There isn't currently any treatment," she answered. My heart sank again. She continued to tell me that my daughter would likely end up in a wheelchair at a young age, and that she would need multiple surgeries to straighten her bones. No running. No playing on the playground. No sports. She likely wouldn't be able to attend school due to the concern that if she got bumped by anyone she could break a bone. She would need to be careful with her body for the rest of her life. She would likely have a lot of pain in her body for the rest of her life. The prognosis and outlook was grim, to put it lightly. And with no treatment in sight, my heart was breaking for my little girl whose future seemingly just went from bright to dark. In that moment I wasn't thinking about anything but the dashed heart of a parent for their child. I hung up the phone.

The moment I hung up the phone, I bawled. I bawled heavily, for days. Every time I thought of it or something reminded me of it, I was instantly in tears. I couldn't even talk about it with friends or family (other than my husband) because the mere mention of it would cause me to burst into tears.

It took me over a year to process and come to grips with the new life that we expected to face with our daughter. Only a parent who's gone through a devastating diagnosis knows what it feels like. It's as if the world comes crashing at your feet and there are so many little shards and slices that you realize you cannot pick them all up and put them back together.

> *It's as if the world comes crashing at your feet and there are so many little shards and slices that you realize you cannot pick them all up and put them back together.*

I would see others moms with their healthy children and wonder if they will ever appreciate just how blessed they are. Things that most parents take for granted, I would guard in my heart with each breath. Even all these years later, I still remember the feeling of hearing that news. All the hopes, dreams and plans we had for her were dashed, *yet*, by the grace of God, I never gave up hope that God could still work a miracle.

I want to encourage you that the story doesn't end there. During that first year after the diagnosis, God put a burning desire in my heart to look for a cure. God knew better. And over that year, He gave me the insatiable desire to search and *find* a solution. Every night, once I tucked my kids into bed, I would go on the computer and research. Anything and everything. Big leads and small. I felt in my spirit that there was treatment out there; I just had to find it. I refused to give up. God works in amazing and mysterious ways and as I think back to those memories of sitting at my kitchen table, looking for answers on the web while plunking the keys of my white MacBook laptop, I can honestly say that I felt God's presence there, guiding me—holding my hand and directing each search result that I came upon. It's that peace that God gives, that cannot be explained in words, but it rested upon me like a soft blanket, night after night as I sat at my laptop.

There were many dead ends. One search came up with bone marrow transplants that had been researched and attempted previously by other patients, but they all failed. There were multiple attempts made to find a cure but none of them fruitful. There was so little known about this rare disease. So little was known about it that when my cousin read about it in her medical encyclopedia, she said the information about it only consisted of one paragraph and even that one paragraph contained minimal information. To this day, when I speak about it with any new doctors we encounter, I have to teach them about it as not a single doctor I've met has ever heard of it. And here I was expecting to find a treatment for a disease that hardly anyone, even specialists, had ever heard of?

But that's what God does. He puts desires in our hearts and He directs our paths. He didn't let me give up. He kept whispering, "One more day. One more search. Trust me."

And I did. God was guiding my steps, each step of the way (Proverbs 16:9) and one year after the diagnosis, we were enrolled in a six-year-long, experimental enzyme replacement treatment study on the opposite side of the country. It involved six years of travel, as frequently as every three weeks in the beginning. All this while raising our second daughter who was a newborn baby, going to university full time to get my teaching degree and everything else in life that doesn't magically just pause when dealing with something like this.

I will say there were a lot of emotions in those six years, a lot of travel and exhaustion, hard decisions, and things I would never want to face again but there was also always a hand holding mine, helping to guide me along and never letting me give up. There were times when it seemed like giving up was the only solution but I can honestly say that the thought never crossed my mind. The verse in Philippians 4:13, that we can do **all** things through Christ who is our strength, became so true and real to me. I cannot ever thank God enough for what He did and has done for me. Because of Him —because He had put that passion in my heart to find treatment, because He pushed me to keep going and because He opened every door I needed opened, I can stand here today and give you the exciting news that my daughter is happy, healthy and her bones are 100% whole. She doesn't have any deficiencies. She plays every single sport in school. She learned to wakeboard last summer. She has scaled walls in rock climbing, been one of the star players on her basketball team, and even with the beautifully active life she leads, she has never broken a single bone since treatment, praise

God! Healing from God comes in many forms and although it involves her taking a simple enzyme, because of that, she lives a perfectly healthy and normal life, much different from what the medical professionals told us she would have. When she embarks on learning something new that's physically active, I often observe myself pausing in a state of gratitude, praying and thanking God for the gift of her healing—thankful that she is able to physically do the things we were told she couldn't. By the grace of God, I am blessed to see the beauty of her life; I don't take things for granted like I would have had we not gone through this. It was such a hard journey but gratitude doesn't even begin to describe what I feel as a mother to see my daughter strong and healthy, living a life of freedom.

Why do I tell you that story? Because in that six-year-long struggle, God never told me why.

And I didn't ask.

I believe God somehow allowed my heart to trust in Him without question, in order to get through the struggle and in doing so, it meant I didn't need to know why. It's funny though, in almost every other area of my life, I am a very curious person. I am *always* asking why. I was probably that persistent toddler who always asked, "But, why?"

Yet, somehow, God gave me the grace not to ask why in all those years and I thank Him from the bottom of my heart for that. Asking why would have affected my ability to trust Him, I have no doubt. And God knew I needed all the grace I could get. I so believe (because I am walking proof of it) that God gives us the grace to endure what we need to endure and I truly believe that part of that is Him giving us supernatural faith to trust in Him, without needing to know why.

Needing to know all the answers seems like it would bring peace but it actually rarely does. Sometimes, God does reveal the 'why' in situations. But many, or most times, He does not. I believe it's because we may not be able to understand, fathom or handle the answer and so, out of love, He just gives us the grace and ability to endure it. Knowing the answer is often overrated and it doesn't change the facts, either. It can also cause you to be angry if you don't agree with the answer to the 'why' question. God is good. If you believe that, then you can also trust that everything He does for you is good, too.

Another reason we are inclined to ask why is because we think if we know the answer, maybe we can help ourselves out of the problem. We can 'help God along' in His timing or in working out the solution. I have a question for you though: How'd that work out for Sarah? In Chapter 16 of Genesis, Sarah thought that she'd help God along in His plan to provide her and Abraham with a child. She convinced her husband to have intercourse with her servant to impregnate her. As you know, in the end, that plan ended with heartache and many lives were ruined because of it.

But don't we do the same? We think we will help God along in His plan and if we know the ending, we can just press 'fast-forward' to the good part. But God doesn't want us to take over.

That's called self-reliance. I don't know if you've found this but it's a lot of work and pressure to take care of yourself, especially when most things are out of your control anyway. We see in the immediate—in our humanness—but God sees the entire picture, from the beginning to the end. He knows the best plan and the best time. He may show you things that you need to do, but it's only because He's created that pathway for you.

No, instead, God tells us all throughout Scripture to trust Him (Proverbs 3:5-6, Psalm 37:4-5, Jeremiah 17:7, Philippians 4:19, John 14:1). Trust. Always. In Proverbs 3:5-6, He asks us to *not lean on our own understanding*. What does that mean? It means that when we try to reason, or figure out the 'why' all the time, we are essentially saying that we think we can figure out the solution ourselves and we don't need God. But is that what we really want? Do we want to be in charge of our lives or do we want to let God be in control? Sometimes I believe we *think* we want to be in charge but the truth is, we have the privilege of being able to trust in God and let Him lead, guide and direct us. His plans for us are *so* good and He knows exactly how to get us there. When we try to be in charge, we are just taking a shot in the dark, like Sarah, and in doing so, we lose out on the bigger and better promises God has in store for us.

Reasoning, finding out the answers, asking why, trying to figure it out: all of those lead to frustration. We cannot figure out God. We can learn about His character, we can spend time in prayer with Him, we can hear the voice of the Holy Spirit speaking to us…we can do all those things but we cannot unravel the mystery of God. It leads to wrong thinking and frustration, but more than that, it leads us away from trusting in Him. I could have wasted hours, weeks, days, months and years worrying about the outcome for my daughter. But it wouldn't have changed the situation or done anything other than rob me of the joy of trusting God. In fact it would have less to stress and worry—both which would rob peace from my life. He is trust*worthy,* and although we can't always guarantee that the struggles will turn out the way we planned or hope for, we can trust that at the root of it all, we serve a God who is *good* and *worthy* of trust. Agonizing over the pain of what my daughter was facing may have distracted me from following God's prompting to search for answers. Instead, God gave me the grace to listen to his voice and trust Him to take care of my daughter, whom He loves even more than I could ever imagine.

Contentment in the Unknown

It is said that trust is one of the most important foundations of a marriage. In order to build a solid marriage, you need to trust the person that you're married to in every area. I would contend that it's the same with our relationship with God. If we don't trust Him, we are losing out on the blessing of walking with God, but we will also spend a lot of time questioning His will, and becoming frustrated with life. We get into 'works of the flesh', meaning we try to do things in our might, will and timing. But that doesn't make us feel any better either. It leads to even more questions and a lot of those roads lead to dead ends.

Something beautiful happened during my journey with God, in those six years of dealing with my daughter's health battle. God gave me the ability to not question Him, or ask Him *why* within the six year journey with my daughter, or even to this day. And I am so thankful for that. But I have not been immune to asking that question in other areas over the years, and it is something I pray about often. I pray for the grace to be able to have that same faith, in all areas of my life.

There have been struggles since then when I have instead chosen to 'lean on my own understanding' rather than on God's. There have also been other times where I have fallen back into the habit of asking why. And it has led to frustration and still-unanswered questions. I have learned not to get angry with myself for asking why but instead put my energy and prayers back into intentionally placing that trust again (and again) in God. It goes back to what I spoke about in Chapter 3—trying to make God follow what we consider is our plan for victory. We get stuck in believing that we know the best way out. We think that we have the optimal plan for how to overcome this problem, and we begin to ask God to do a, b and c.

One thing I've often thought about is the fact that Paul was able to learn how to patiently trust and wait on God, despite his circumstances. That has recently really struck me. I don't think that means that we can't pray and ask God to remove the hard circumstances because I absolutely believe that we can. But I do think we need to pray and ask for God's will, not ours. Keep coming back to trust in our God who is at work in our circumstances. And as we wait in faith, making the *choice* that if we must endure it, that we would endure it with faith, trust, hope and grace. I believe that if we pray for God's *will*, we can rest in knowing He knows just what to do and if that means fixing or taking away the problem, He will! And we can have that rest *while* we wait for the victory, not just after the victory comes.

Paul said in Philippians 4:11 that he had "*learned* the secret to being content in any situation." That has been my prayer for the past four years. Every day. Every day, I ask God to show me and teach me how to be content no matter what my situation. It doesn't mean I don't want things to go smoothly 100% the time, because while that would be lovely, it's also not realistic. And if my attitude and my joy are *based and contingent* on my situations, I am setting myself up for failure, because circumstances will not always be favourable. There just *will* be struggles in life. Loved ones pass away. Jobs get lost. Friends have arguments. Things happen in life that are hard. We know that Jesus said, "in this world you will have trouble," but He also tells us He will be with us, that He's overcome it, and that He *will be with us always* (John 16:33, Matthew 28:20). We don't have to do it alone. Isn't that such a big blessing!? Do we realize what a privilege that is? I mean, it's *huge!*

Note that Paul says He has **learned** the secret to being content. This wasn't something that he just fell into, and it wasn't overnight. He had to work at it. Look at some of the trials and struggles he endured. We don't know about all of Paul's trials but based on the accounts we do know of, I can say he ought to be revered for his hopeful attitude and thankfulness to God in all things. He had to endure some pretty hefty trials in order to *learn* how to be content in all situations. But remember, he didn't do it alone; God was with him through it all and working it for good in Paul's life. It's amazing what good can come from trials when God gets involved. The same is true for us: God will work good out of our trials when we give it to Him and surrender ourselves, allowing Him to do His will in our lives.

There are stories all throughout history of strong believers who have undergone intense trials yet God gave them the strength to endure it. Allow me to share with you an excerpt from a powerful story about a Holocaust survivor, Corrie Ten Boom.

Giving Thanks in All Circumstances

"Corrie and Betsie Ten Boom were courageous, compassionate Dutch Christians who helped harbour Jews from the Nazis in Holland during World War 2. After the sisters were arrested for doing so, they were imprisoned at Ravensbruck, a German concentration camp. This is part of their story.

In their barracks, they were shown to a series of massive square platforms, stacked three levels high and placed so close together that people had to walk single-file to pass between them. Rancid straw was scattered over the platforms, which served as communal beds for hundreds of women. Corrie and Betsie found they could not sit upright on their own platform without hitting their heads on the deck above them. They lay back, struggling against nausea that swept over them from the reeking straw.

Suddenly Corrie started up, striking her head on the cross-slats above. Something had bitten her leg. "Fleas!" she cried. "Betsie, the place is swarming with them!" Descending from the platform and edging down a narrow aisle, they made their way to a patch of light. "Here! And here another one!" Corrie wailed. "Betsie, how can we live in such a place?"

"Show us. Show us how," Betsie said matter-of-factly. It took Corrie a moment to realize that her sister was praying. "Corrie!" Betsie then exclaimed excitedly. "He's given us the answer! Before we asked, as He always does! In the Bible this morning. Where was it? Read that part again!"

Corrie checked to make sure no guards were nearby, then drew from a pouch a small Bible she had managed to smuggle into the concentration camp. "It was in First Thessalonians," she said, finding the passage in the feeble light. "Here it is: 'Comfort the frightened, help the weak, be patient with everyone. See that none of you repays evil for evil, but always seek to do good to one another and to all. Rejoice always, pray constantly, give thanks in all circumstances; for this is the will of God in Christ Jesus ...'"(1 Thessalonians 5:14-18).

"That's it!" Betsie interrupted. "That's His answer. 'Give thanks in all circumstances!' That's what we can do. We can start right now to thank God for every single thing about this barracks!"

Corrie stared at her incredulously, then around at the dark, foul-smelling room. "Such as?" she inquired.

"Such as being assigned here together." Corrie bit her lip. "Oh yes, Lord Jesus!"

"Such as what you're holding in your hands." Corrie looked down at the Bible.

"Yes! Thank You, dear Lord, that there was no inspection when we entered here! Thank You for all the women, here in this room, who will meet You in these pages."

"Yes," agreed Betsie. "Thank You for the very crowding here. Since we're packed so close, that many more will hear!"

She looked at her sister expectantly and prodded, "Corrie!"

"Oh, all right. Thank You for the jammed, crammed, stuffed, packed, suffocating crowds."

"Thank you," Betsie continued on serenely, "for the fleas and for …"

That was too much for Corrie. She cut in on her sister: "Betsie, there's no way even God can make me grateful for a flea."

"'Give thanks in all circumstances,'" Betsie corrected. "It doesn't say, 'in pleasant circumstances.' Fleas are part of this place where God has put us." So they stood between the stacks of bunks and gave thanks for fleas, though on that occasion Corrie thought Betsie was surely wrong.

As the weeks passed, Betsie's health weakened to the point that, rather than needing to go out on work duty each day, she was permitted to remain in the barracks and knit socks together with other seriously-ill prisoners. She was a lightning fast knitter and usually had her daily sock quota completed by noon. As a result, she had hours each day she could spend moving from platform to platform reading the Bible to fellow prisoners. She was able to do *this undetected as the guards never seemed to venture far into the barracks.*

One evening when Corrie arrived back at the barracks Betsie's eyes were twinkling. "You're looking extraordinarily pleased with yourself," Corrie told her.

"You know we've never understood why we had so much freedom in the big room," Betsie said, referring to the part of the barracks where the sleeping platforms were. "Well—I've found out. This afternoon there was confusion in my knitting group about sock sizes, so we asked the supervisor to come and settle it. But she wouldn't. She wouldn't step through the door and neither would the guards. And you know why?" Betsie could not keep the triumph from her voice as she exclaimed, "Because of the fleas! That's what she said: 'That place is crawling with fleas!'"

Corrie's mind raced back to their first hour in the barracks. She remembered Betsie bowing her head and thanking God for creatures that Corrie could see no use for" (Christie).

The story of Corrie and Bestie is an incredibly brave and sobering story. Someone and something to aspire to—true faith and true ability to trust God in all circumstances. Although we would never wish to be in a concentration camp by any stretch of the imagination, the reality is that even in our hardest struggles, we can choose to be thankful and content, seeing what God *is* doing with spiritual perspective rather than looking at the situation with our human understanding.

I want to make crystal clear the importance of putting reasoning away and letting the Lord lead you to a place of leaning on *His* understanding instead of your own. Have faith, and trust in the fact that God *does* know the way out (1 Corinthians 10:13), that He *is* at work and that He *will* lead you down the path you're supposed to be on. Once you let go of needing to know all the answers; once you let go of the 'why' and choose to put your faith and trust in God, you'll be amazed at the shackles that fall off. You can begin to live life with abandonment to yourself and complete freedom in knowing God has a plan and He is at work for your *good* (Romans 8:28).

CHAPTER 5

Comparison is a Killer

One day, a glass of air and a glass of water were comparing themselves to each other. They wanted to prove who was more superior.

"I am superior because I give air to the lungs and help humans breathe," said the glass of air, proudly beaming as he puffed up his chest and calmly sat down with his nose pointed high in the air.

"Yes, but I give humans the hydration they need to keep all their systems healthy," the glass of water chirped back.

"I am needed moment by moment. You can be avoided for up to three days," boasted the glass of air.

"Ah yes, but with all the air in the world and no water, it would do no good," the glass of air happily beamed back.

"But without me, humans would die."

"Same with me. Humans would certainly die without me."

The glass of water and the glass of air realized that no matter how much they compared themselves, neither was superior. They were equal, yet so very different. One could not imitate the other and they both needed to work in harmony together. No matter how *superior one seemed to the other with an isolated purpose, one could not function without the other. They both served different purposes but they were both needed in order to accomplish sustaining life for a human.*

One of the things that will drive you towards bitterness, resentment and pain is the tiny but powerful behaviour of comparing yourself to someone else: to their looks, their situation in life, or their level of struggle in life. I'm sure we've all done it; I know I have. That pesky saying, *the grass is always greener on the other side,* couldn't be more true. It's easy to think everyone else's life is easier than your own. It's easy to begin comparing your circumstances to someone else's without even knowing it. I'm not just talking about their looks or their house or how much money they make; I'm talking specifically about when we compare our lives to someone else in relation to their level of struggle (or perhaps, lack thereof). It's easy to think that others don't deal with hard things and that they have it so easy—"they" being anyone other than you.

When you're in the middle of the battle, it can seem that everyone else is on the sidelines, sprawled out over a lounge chair, cheerfully sipping lemonade. It can appear that they've got it all together, especially when you pop onto social media and see manufactured, picture-perfect lives. People don't generally post their bed-head photos. No; they post a calculated, edited photo of themselves, perfectly posed with a charmingly flattering filter. I'm not saying that we have to post all of the hard things in our days either, but I am saying that often what we see on social media is not at all representative of people's real, everyday lives. What we see online is a filtered life. It's unbalanced. We have to know that going in, otherwise it can start to feel like everyone else has a rosy life and ours is far less ____ (fill in the blank…exciting, tidy, perfect, etc).

That word: perfect. It really should be eradicated from the English language as it does not serve us well as humans, because it's unattainable. How often do we hear the word perfect in a day? Probably a dozen times. "Oh that outfit looks perfect on you!", "You got a perfect score", "Practice makes perfect," or "Her children are so perfect." It becomes something to measure ourselves with, yet the perception of truth has only a fraction of reality attached to it. The moment sin entered the world, the possibly of perfect was gone. There is only One who is perfect, and He is God.

But in the culture we live in, perfect is something that people seem to try to attain. The perfect body. The perfect job. The perfect house. The perfect relationship. The perfect family. Perfect, perfect, perfect. When did perfect become the standard to measure ourselves by? We are setting ourselves up for failure each time!

Yet, the fact still remains. Perfection is being pursued by so many in the world. Marriages are being broken because of it, lives are being taken because of it and so many other terrible things happen in the pursuit of perfection.

You may be saying, "I get that, but I know I'll never be perfect. I just want to have it better than what it is right now." And that's okay. It's okay to be hopeful for the future. That's biblical! The problem lies in when we begin comparing ourselves to others and their lives. When we start to think they've got it 'perfect' and we are stuck with perfect's ugly step-sister, 'struggle'.

One thing I've learned is that no one has it perfect. That's a pure fact. We all strive for joy and peace and happiness in our lives, and we might have those things. But perfect isn't the word to describe them. Everyone—men and women, old and young—have their own struggles that they deal with and in that, we can share in their journey. We can pray for them and love them as they struggle. We don't need to compare our journey to theirs. When we compare ourselves to others, we are essentially saying that we aren't good enough, or that our circumstances aren't good enough. We begin to negate the work that God is doing in our lives. God made only one you. And He only made one of everyone else. He has a special and unique plan for your life, just like He does for every other person's life. Comparing ourselves to someone else is saying to God that you don't think He knew or knows what He's doing in our lives. We negate the trust and hope in Him when we compare.

Of course we don't do that intentionally, but when we continue to compare ourselves to others, it opens the door for the enemy to plant seeds of resentment, bitterness, frustration, and possibly the most damaging of all, feeling pity for ourselves.

Pity is a slippery slope for both believers and unbelievers. Remember when you were a child, and you scraped your knee or got hurt, and you'd run to your mom or dad, or the closest adult and show them your wound and they would say something like, "Oh hunny, you poor thing. Let me help you." It felt good. You felt like you were being taken care of and that someone cared. In that moment, what you needed was a hug and a Bandaid, and you were thankful there was someone there to give it to you.

Or other times, when you would fall and get hurt, you held it together with no tears and were brave...but the moment you saw your mom or dad, or whoever your caretaker was, you weren't able to keep those tears in any longer and immediately they spilled out of you like a rushing dam. It was because you knew that you could let your guard down and just be transparent with how you felt with no fear of judgement. You could let it out.

That is what our relationship with God can be. And maybe it is for you. You run into His arms when you fall and hurt yourself, knowing He will take care of you and bind up your wounds; "He heals the brokenhearted and bandages their wounds" (Psalm 147:3, NLT). You run into His presence, pour out your heart to Him and let Him comfort you.

What does that have to do with pity? In the example of a child who falls and goes and runs to their parent to fix their wound, the sense of their parent having sympathy fo them is endearing and beautiful when it's properly placed. But when we instead feel pity for ourselves, it doesn't allow the Lord to step in and work in us. It turns into self-reliance and trying to take care of ourselves. It says in 1 Peter 5:7, you are supposed to "give all your worries and cares to God, for He cares about you." What a privilege as believers!

Rather, when we feel pity for ourselves we also take on the responsibility of taking care of our own wounds. We never stop God from working because He can absolutely work without our invitation; *however,* I would maintain that we can inhibit what He does because of our free will. If we are choosing to rely on ourselves instead of Him, we are essentially saying that we can take care of ourselves. We aren't allowing God to come in and do what He wants to do and we instead say, "I've got this," taking our care into our own hands.

I don't know about you, but I can't take care of myself and all my needs on my own. I fully recognize that if I'm going to do anything in life, I need God's help each day. Sometimes, when I begin to have pity on myself, I'm pushing away the hand that God offers to help me up and help me out. He is Sovereign and in control and I'm positive there are many times when I've seen Him step in, in spite of me trying to take care of myself. He ultimately will still choose the best for us, even when we are too stubborn or unaware to ask for it. His plans for us are always good (Jeremiah 29:11). For that we should daily be thankful.

I want to emphasize how much we need to stop comparing ourselves to others and their lives in order to quantify what we are going through. Everyone has their struggles, even those who don't look like they are or ever share about them. We need to keep our eyes focused on what God has for us, trusting Him in the process and letting Him know that we are relying on *Him* to take care of us, not ourselves. Give God verbal acknowledgement, telling Him you trust Him and that you're giving Him your struggles and your cares. Give Him the thanks He deserves and watch the amazing things He does in your life.

Leaning on Each Other

People don't often share about their struggles, which draw us to the ideas of transparency and openness. I think it's important to preamble these concepts by saying that I don't believe we should be dumping all our problems on those around us. There are certain things that are between you and God, that should only be spoken between you and God, or perhaps someone trustworthy like your parent, your spouse or a very close friend. Understanding this takes discernment. However, I will say, that I think authenticity and transparency are fading away in our society and one negative effect of that is people are believing that they're the only ones with struggles.

Evidence of this has come out in the media at times, in waves. Issues are brought to light and dealt with such as the *Me, Too* movement, or the *Black Lives Matter* movement, and many others. Then, all of the sudden, a bunch of public figures come out of the woodworks, relaying the message that, "Yes, that happened to me to!" This is an example of the need for authenticity and transparency in our society. It's now at the point where hidden (but common) issues need to be broadcast publicly in order for individuals and society to be honest about what's going on in their lives, or to stand in solidarity to bring about change. It shouldn't take such a public appeal to the masses for these issues to be discussed and dealt with. These kinds of issues should be talked about and dealt with as part being a community, a tribe: a village.

If, as a society in general, we were more honest about what we are going through, there wouldn't be as great a need for public appeal calling transparency into these kinds of struggles. If society as a whole shared more of their hearts and struggles with those around them, there would be more opportunity for healing. There would be more prayer. There would be more brothers and sisters in Christ stepping up and helping. There would be more breakthrough.

I have to say that although I want to see even more of this across the nations, I believe that for the most part this is an area where the church excels. I'm not going to say every denomination or every church has mastered this but I'm going to make a generalization here: I would love to see the church become even more approachable for anyone, regardless of where they are at in their journey, to just walk in and seek help. Ideally, the church is a place where people who lack the support of friends or family in their lives, or who just need more support, can come and experience a listening heart and receive prayer. By opening up to someone who's praying for them or by even silently receiving prayer, they are able to give it to God, bring it into His marvellous light and begin starting the journey of healing. I love that the Church (in general) has open arms to say to those who need it, 'We're here. We are listening. We are ready to pray with and for you and help shoulder this with you, as we give it to God." I think that altar calls and prayer nights are such a blessing in our lives, and so important. They take issues or struggles that lie in the shadows and bring them into the light of God.

If we would strive as a society—or let's be more practical here — if *you* would strive to be more open and transparent about your struggles in a healthy way, sharing in the reality of everyday life with those around you, it may not only be an open door to let someone else share something that's been heavy on their heart or that they need prayer for, but it also brings a sense of normalcy to those around you, showing them that struggle is an inevitable part of life that we all deal with at different times. It helps normalize the reality of struggle rather than painting a picture of perfection that's rampant in the world today.

I personally know the struggle with transparency from the process I went through in writing my previous book. It is not easy to be open about the struggles we face. But as hard as it was to be open and vulnerable about my own personal journey with anxiety, the passages where I shared personal stories of my own struggles and victory were the passages that spoke most to those reading it. The vulnerability in human struggle is something we all connect with. The readers felt like they weren't alone. They felt like it was okay to be honest about it. Best of all, they realized that my testimony could be their testimony, that they could overcome struggle with God's help and begin to walk in freedom. Stepping out in openness, was the springboard that launched others into a new level of freedom. Even in this book, as I've shared some deeply honest and personal stories, it's only by God's strength and courage that I am able to share these stories. I am fully aware that I could be judged by them or criticized but I don't let that stop me because I know, that I know, that I know, that God has called me to be vulnerable and open, no matter what others may think. Testimony breeds testimony and I believe authenticity is also contagious. My prayer is that as you connect with these stories, you'll see that we all make mistakes and have struggles, too. God uses the willing, not the perfect. Share your personal stories. Share what God has done and believe that He can do it again!

Let's look at an example that Magda Murawska shared about comparison and our human nature.

Comparing pickles to wrenches

"I hope that I am not alone when I recall the following scenario – Sitting at a table with friends, I listen to them discuss their accounts of job promotions and various exciting life experiences. Happy and proud of my friends' accomplishments, I find myself comparing my own life to theirs. It's almost an involuntary act, one that has been honed with years of practice. My comparison begins in the calm waters of commonalities, but quickly veers into the more dangerous high tide of comparisons, as I began to negatively compare what's lacking in my life based on what is present in theirs. I soon hear the thoughts of "I should be farther ahead in my career," "I should be doing this," "I should be doing that," etc. I've entered the 'Sea of Shoulds' – an unpredictable place, like the Bermuda Triangle, where few come out unscathed."

[…]

"By comparing ourselves to others we're negating our own road and demanding that the past be different than what it was. The demands we place on ourselves to be like those we're comparing ourselves to may sometimes be motivations for change, however they are more likely to lead to feelings of diminished self-worth."

"We as humans are too complex to be rated or described by a phrase or two. We are similarly too complex to rate ourselves based on the comparison to another, complex human being," (Murawska).

Magda Murawska accurately describes the struggle we all face. The ability to compare ourselves with one another is almost involuntary. It happens quickly and sometimes without awareness. But what we can begin to do is when we recognize that we are comparing ourselves, we can remember that God created us uniquely for a purpose and for a plan. Psalm 57:2 says, "I cry out to God Most High, to God who fulfills His purpose for me," and in Psalm 139:16 it says, "all the days ordained for me were written in your book before one of them came to be."

Your struggle will be used to make you strong in different ways than someone else. Let their struggle be theirs to overcome and grow from, and let yours be yours. He can and does use the lessons from hardships to shape you uniquely into a person that will be used to help others in their struggles. Like a glob of clay that is moulded and shaped into a beautiful piece of pottery, let God mould you from the clay, let these struggles shape and form you into the person you are today because "we know that all things work together for the good of those who love Him and are called according to His purpose" (Romans 8:28). Don't compare one piece of pottery to the other, but rather let the entire collection of pottery be adored.

If you find that you are comparing yourself to someone else, take a moment and read Psalm 139. Take another moment and pray and ask God to remind you of His love. It's important to remember that God made you unique and special. He has a purpose for you on this earth. If you're feeling like you're aimlessly wandering, don't waste more time feeling that way. Ask God what He wants to use you for. Ask Him to reveal His purposes and plans for you. Perhaps He will tell you the entire picture, or He may just give you one step at a time in the right direction. Both are good. Trust each step as He shows you and know that He has good plans for you!

CHAPTER 6

Healing from the Past

"If you spend time judging and criticizing people, you will not have time to heal from your pain or brokenness. You cannot love yourself when you judge or criticize others who are created in God's image and after His Likeness...in which you are also created. Love cannot operate from a space of pain. Love and hurt cannot reside in the same space."
    -Kemi Sogunle

For me to stand here and say that I can speak from a place of knowledge about a tragically painful past would be grossly unfair to those who have struggled more greatly than I have. I desire openness from others and I will be open in telling you that you don't need to break out the wine and violin for me. Although we all face struggles in our lives, I'd be exaggerating the story of my life if I said it was tragic. It's not. I grew up in a loving Christian home, and even though there are some things that I had to work through as an adult, it was pretty great. I married the love of my life at a young age and soon we had two beautiful daughters together. Yes, we have had many struggles as everyone does, some more monumental than others, such as my daughter's health journey. But relatively speaking, I cannot complain or try to convince you that the life I've been given has been tragic. Perhaps part of that is perspective.

Those who know me well have said to me at different points in some of the struggles I've faced that they don't know how I've come through various trials with a smile. When I look back at the mountains I've faced, the truth is that there are some pretty big giants in there. I mean, yes, our life has been blessed, but I guess it's not as simple as some that we know, either. It's had its seasons of hardships and difficulties, some that have had moments where it felt too great to conquer, some that felt like it would be the wave that would sink us, but none of those have ever been too great to bear because God has walked us through each one.

Sometimes I look at those around us whose lives seem simpler than ours and I wonder what it would be like. My husband and I are dreamers at heart. We love to push the limits on the opportunities life can bring and we often dare to dream about bigger things in the future. Simple has never really been our thing. Most of the time it's great because we get to see and do things we would never do if we weren't ambitious. God has given both of us a great deal of determination. Perhaps that determination is part of His gift to us, so that we can endure with fortitude the trials that have come our way. But there are times when I wonder if we should just cash in the chips and take a back seat— you know—coast for a while.

Usually that thought comes to greet me in the middle of a trial. It comes when I'm feeling the weight of the problem on me.

it all and while I'm in the middle of a struggle. I often think that the way to accomplish that is by kissing ambition goodbye and burrowing away like a squirrel in its wintery slumber, shutting the world out for a couple months while settling into a nice, warm, cozy hole in the earth.

It's in those times when determination can feel like a drawback to my personality. Sometimes, I don't *want* to be the strong one. Sometimes, it feels like it would be easier to be a sweet, quiet, passive person with not so much as even an opinion to stand on. Sometimes having fortitude and endurance is a lot of hard work. It can feel like a defect to be 'put together' while under pressure, while others seem to be getting an easy road in life. When you're in the middle of the storm, the pressure to be brave can be daunting. But God gives us only what we can handle (1 Corinthians 10:13) and if He gave me the qualities of endurance and fortitude (which He did), then I need to stay focused and run my race. Not everyone can ride in the back-seat of life. The doers get things done but it can often come at a cost. During these times is also when God reminds me that I need to stop trying to do it on my own—that I need to give Him the control. This is something I still need to be reminded of—something I'm still working on and thankfully something He's *still working* on in me, everyday.

I gave you that preamble because I want to be transparent about the next part I am going to share. It will be easier for you to grasp the full picture of who I am, and part of what my story is as you read further. Although my past isn't riddled with what most would consider to be tragedy: no need to flee my homeland due to war, no abusive past; there have been some significant struggles along the way, and I believe that it's okay to acknowledge that each person's struggle or pain is worth addressing. Society tends to go to extremes when it comes to less life-altering struggles: we either tend to belittle the small pains, or we over exaggerate them.

For example, a little boy who has a paper cut and throws himself on the floor, reeling for attention can get a pity party thrown in his honour by the doting adults around him. Yet something as damaging as being teased or bullied in school can be seen as part of life, when in fact it could have long-lasting and damaging effects on that child for the rest of her life. It seems that in our world today, the gauge is broken on how to appropriately deal with pain.

Pain is a part of life. It just is. I wish it wasn't. I wish that the gripping pain of death would never befall anyone I love. Or that automobile accidents ceased to exist, or suicides. Or that war was only something of the storybooks: fictitious and imaginary. How lovely would that be? But that's not the way life works, and when dealing with pain, God can equip us with the tools we need to get through it by relying on Him. Part of that process is looking at the past as a blueprint for some of the pain that we carry with us today.

The teasing experienced by the girl in school may be disregarded as nothing to be concerned about when she's a child, but it could turn into issues, that if left unnoticed, could wreak havoc on her self-worth as she grows up. It could lead low self-esteem or feelings of worthlessness, causing her to try to fill that void by seeking the wrong kind of attention from others. Painful experiences and the emotions that come with them don't always escalate, but they often do, and the importance of immediately dealing with them is paramount. The pain these experiences cause can often go unnoticed until one day, the pain resurfaces, seemingly out of nowhere. And until the root of the issue is acknowledged and dealt with, one cannot move forward in a healthy manner. This is an example of what the world may not label 'tragic,' but for that girl, it's a foundational issue that would need to be addressed before healing can take place. We have to stop minimizing the effects of the roots of pain in our lives and start realizing that that's one key role that the Holy Spirit is here for: to counsel us and bring healing into those hurting places.

As Kemi Sogunle writes in her book, *Beyond the Pain*, "If you are busy focusing on the falling bricks, you will never realize that they are truly stepping stones you need to cross over to the next phase of your life" (Sogunle)

I love that! What a poetic description of the journey that we all must face. We need to pause sometimes, and look at the pain that we are struggling with, asking God to show us where the root of it began, before we can move forward in freedom. We cannot ignore the past or it will hold us back from the future. We cannot go forward unless we address the root cause of the issue. Failing to do so will result in all the effort being fruitless. However, constantly looking back to the past prevents us from moving forward; **but** like Kemi Segunle says, sometimes you need to recognize the pain from the past and use that as a stepping stone to rebuild your future, taking the time to address the issues and pains from your past and seeking to find out if they link to your present. Ask God. Even if it's painful to pray about or think about. Spiritually speaking, you are not fully restored if you are still walking with a limp.

Think about a gaping wound. If it's big or deep enough, it will require stitches to be properly sealed. If you neglect to stitch it, the wound keeps opening up. It may start to heal a little but then the next time it gets bumped or stretched, it opens again. That pattern keeps repeating itself until it's dealt with—until it's stitched. Much in the same way, the wounds from our past or even our present that we don't deal with cannot heal properly, and all it takes is a little bump and the wound can become reopened. The pain returns and it hurts all over again each time it's reopened.

> *Spiritually speaking, you are not fully restored if you are still walking with a limp.*

The pain in our lives doesn't have to be hugely tragic to still cause damage. It can be an accumulation of small things or it can be a common thread of a reoccurring situation. I have had to go through some restoration healing with God for some traumas that have occurred in my life; they may not be considered traumatic to some, but they were painful for me, nonetheless. And yet, something traumatic to someone else may not even phase me. We have to be kind to ourselves in not judging our pain but instead opening it up to God to be transparent and deal with it. Ask God to show you what you need to heal from in your past or your present. Open your entire heart up to Him. The pain doesn't need to be big to be painful. A paper cut is one of the smallest injuries you can see but anyone who's had one knows it can hurt a lot. Now, imagine if you've had 25 paper cuts in a row; they can add up to a lot of pain and hurt. Although the saying, "death by a thousand paper cuts," is made to sound poetic, the truth behind it is more poignant than we give it credit for. It means that when a lot of little things add up, they can turn into something very big. In the same way, we have to address whether a painful situation, or an accumulation of painful situations, has led to trauma, which leads to distorted thinking.

Trauma comes in many forms. I will never understand some of the tragedies that others endure. I cannot fathom the depth of pain that resides in someone losing a child to suicide or murder. I can't imagine the pain felt by women who've been raped or abused. Those traumas far outweigh anything I've endured and I don't want to belittle the trauma restoration steps I outline as being a one-size-fits all. Those kinds of traumas may need to be dealt with more seriously with a Christian counsellor and some restorative, declarative prayer. Trauma isn't just psychological, it's also very spiritual. The enemy has an open door through trauma. It allows him to come in and speak lies and distort the truth even further. If it's not dealt with immediately, roots begin to grow. Trauma like that is serious and needs serious intervention. Perhaps praying through it is a start but likely there needs to be more intervention than that. Seek out someone who you know can pray for you, to declare healing and restoration and will continue to pray for you as you navigate through the restoration process. It could be a friend, someone you know through church, a pastor, a Christian counsellor, or any of those. But hear this so clearly: don't minimize your trauma and assume you can just do it on your own. You can't ignore the past or the pain and hope it will go away. It typically won't just go away on its own.

On the other hand, there are smaller traumas that occur in our lives which we also tend to minimize. If someone has been really hurt by a friend, especially if it's seemingly malicious, it can take time for the wound to heal. Forgiveness would need to take place and perhaps a conversation, if necessary or possible. However, if that isn't properly dealt with, and things move on without addressing the issue, the next time that friend does something unkind, all the same feelings and hurt will resurface, and it may take even longer to move past the pain the second or third or fourth time. This is an example of what would not be considered a tragic situation yet still requires dealing with the hurt. By discounting the pain and not properly dealing with it, it could potentially ruin a friendship or cause someone to carry a lot of hurt and pain around with them that they bring into future relationships. Pain doesn't just go away—it stays with you until it's dealt with.

Trauma Distorts Our Thinking

Trauma is a large part of what keeps people stuck in their pain. It's also a large part of what the enemy uses to bring confusion and anger towards God. Trauma is one of those things that cannot be ignored or assumed that it will just 'resolve itself.' Trauma distorts thinking. And distorted thinking is a perfect entry way for the enemy to come in and try to confuse you, as well as make you believe things that aren't true.

Think of a pair of reading glasses. If you look through them, they magnify the image you're looking at. It's clear and they do the job. But what if you were to line up and look through four pairs of reading glasses? The image would now be distorted, out of proportion and unidentifiable. It's the same with trauma. In the example above, one pair of reading glasses represents reality without trauma. You can see things clearly. But four pairs of reading glasses lined up represents how you see things through the eyes of trauma. It's distorted and you cannot see things clearly.

It's important to address any issues, whether they are large traumas or little ones, with the One who heals the broken-hearted and binds up all their wounds (Psalm 147:3). He doesn't want to us to live out our days in brokenness. He wants to restore us and make us whole. Unearthing and dealing with past traumas doesn't seem appealing, but it is freeing. You can begin to finally close the wound and let it heal.

The following steps are a practical guide to help you begin to address the trauma and start to heal from it. I encourage you to do it, either with another believer, or alone or with a spouse/trusted friend, or a Christian counsellor. I would do these six steps in order, and repeat these steps for each trauma or painful experience. If these steps are not enough to heal the more extreme traumas, please take the time to seek out professional help via a Christian counsellor or a pastor (often many churches offer free pastoral counselling). But always begin by inviting the Holy Spirit to lead and guide you. He will speak to you and walk you through.

Trauma Restoration Steps

1. Acknowledge out loud or journal about the traumatic or painful situation. Write down the situation as it happened in order, your feelings about it, and the details.

2. What has it changed about your thinking? List all answers.
   *example: it made me fearful of...
   I believed this (lie) about God,
   I believed that I could or couldn't _____

3. In reading your answers from #2, circle the key emotions that were triggers. (Ex: fear, doubt, lack of faith, hope)

4. Go through the list of words or sentences that you underlined; pray, ask and receive forgiveness in areas where you've doubted, had lack of faith or believed wrong things about God.

5. What does the Word of God say about the triggers you listed (fear, doubt, anger, worry)? *If you don't know where to find verses on these words, type in the keyword and the word 'verses or scripture' into a search engine (ex: verses about fear). Write them down. Then take some time to read through and study those verses. There is no rush; this may take some time, perhaps a few weeks.

6. Meditate on the verses you found, and pray. Continually. When you feel tempted or when you feel weak, anytime you need a reminder. Pray and read the Word. Rinse and repeat, continually.

Let's look at an example to demonstrate how your answers might look.

We will use a fictional example of the trauma of being teased in school. (The following details are fictional and intended for exemplary purposes only.)

Acknowledge out loud or journal about the traumatic or painful situation. Write down the situation as it happened in order, your feelings about it, and the details:

1. When I was in grade 5, I was teased a lot about how I smelled. My dad was a smoker and my mom didn't mind the smell, so all of my clothes smelled like smoke. It was usually three girls that would tease me: Cindy, Jane and Mary. They would call me names like (____) and (_____). I would often eat my lunch alone in the back corner of the room where no one sat. I was very lonely. The name calling didn't stop all through elementary school. When I got to high school, the name calling stopped but the damage was done. I had a reputation for being smelly and I only had one friend who accepted me. This affected

my self-esteem and I always felt like I was less than everyone else. I began to smoke in grade 9 to help deal with the anxiety. I figured I was already accused of smelling bad, so why not?

_____

What has it changed about your thinking? List all answers.
　example: it made me fearful of...
　I believed this (lie) about God,
　I believed that I could or couldn't _____

2. Now that I live on my own, I am obsessive about cleaning. I am fearful of any and all smells in my home. I don't smoke anymore and I don't have any pets or anything that could cause odour. I am afraid to have anyone over for fear of even the smallest scent of anything so I spend a lot of time alone. It's changed my personality and my thinking. I believe that God could have rescued me from that situation and I am angry that He didn't. I am afraid to let anyone close to me. I am embarrassed about my past. I don't talk about it ever. It's changed my relationships as I haven't had a boyfriend or a close friend in years. At my job I keep air fresheners everywhere and I'm afraid that if I don't, something will smell and the fear or someone talking about me is too scary to endure. This has made me believe that I am not worthy of friendship or love and that my scent is more important than who I am. I love God but I am

afraid to trust Him to take care of me.

In reading your answers from #2, circle the key emotions that were triggers. (Ex: fear, doubt, lack of faith, hope)

3. Now that I live on my own, I am obsessive about cleaning. I am _fearful_ of any and all smells in my home. I don't smoke anymore and I don't have any pets or anything can could cause odour. I am _afraid_ to have anyone over for _fear_ of even the smallest scent of anything so I spend a lot of time alone. It's changed my personality and my thinking. <u>I believe that God could have rescued me from that situation</u> and I am _angry_ that He didn't. I am _afraid_ to let anyone close to me. I am _embarrassed_ about my past. I don't talk about it ever. <u>Its changed my relationships</u> as I haven't had a boyfriend or a close friend in years. At my job I keep air fresheners everywhere and I'm _afraid_ that if I don't, something will smell and the _fear_ or someone talking about me is too _scary_ to endure. <u>This has made me believe that I am not worthy of friendship or love and that my scent is more important than who I am.</u> I love God but <u>I am afraid to trust Him to take care of me.</u>

What does the Word of God say about the triggers you listed (fear, doubt, anger, worry)?

5. **Fear: verses about fear**
   - 2 Timothy 1:7—For God has not given us a Spirit of fear but of power, love and a sound mind.
   - Isaiah 41:10—"So do not fear, for I am with you; do not be dismayed, for I am your God. I will strengthen you and help you; I will uphold you with my righteous right hand."
   - Etc

This is not a one-shoe-fits-all scenario. This is not intended to be a cure-all. This is a guide that will help you start working through the steps of pain or trauma, but if you're feeling stuck or unable to start, perhaps doing these steps with a trusted friend or a Christian counsellor, or a pastor may be a better option for you. There is no shame in seeking help if the trauma or pain is too difficult to navigate on your own. Everyone's journey is going to look different. Find what works for you and be proud of the fact that you're moving forward and not staying stuck in the pain of the past. Remember, moving forward is key, no matter how small the baby steps may be. Healing from past pains and traumas can be challenging, but it's the only way you can begin to move forward.

CHAPTER 7

When you Least Expect it

So a 'thing' happened a year ago. I was miraculously healed. Yes. You may be wondering what that has to do with the question of God's care for us. You may be wondering, why, if I have already received healing in my life, would I dare ask for more. Perhaps it seems unfair that I received healing, while you're in the midst of a storm. It may seem entitled for me to even consider asking for more healing when many go an entire lifetime without receiving any healing. I would argue, many go an entire lifetime with out receiving healing that they *know of*. I believe God heals all the time, saves us from disasters and death, all while we keep going on our merry way, unaware of angels around us.

But that may not convince you that I should be asking for more from God. Yes, I am bold and I will show you why that's exactly how God tells us to be.

> "Let us then approach God's throne of grace with confidence, so that we may receive mercy and find grace to help us in our time of need" Hebrews 4:16 (NIV).

I'll tell you why I still pray and ask: because I don't believe God only honours *some* of His promises. I decided a long time ago that I must either believe the entire Bible or none of it. I cannot pick and choose what I think is relevant or true and disregard the rest. I believe it all. In doing so, I believe God's promise to me that by His stripes we are healed. And so I continue to pray for healing for my knee and any other parts of me that need it—spiritually, emotionally or physically. But I won't go any further without telling you the story of my own, personal touch from God.

What do I mean when I talk about healing? I am talking about a miraculous touch from God that repaired something in my body. There are many accounts of healings in the Bible but also throughout history and in our present time.

I remember the moment clearly. It was in the wee hours of the morning, at 3:00 am, June 26th, 2019. I was actually immobile in my bed because of a bad motor biking accident I was in, two weeks prior (yes, that's the incident that caused the knee injury). I was on crutches and each night it was a big procedure to get myself ready for bed. After icing it all day, I would gently lift my injured leg and carefully bend it on the pillow before drifting off to sleep. Thankfully though, I've always been a pretty good sleeper and even though I would wake up to turn over and adjust my leg, I was still sleeping quite well at night.

As I said, it was 3:00 am on the dot. I had suddenly awoken, almost as if someone was nudging my shoulder to wake me. I woke up and I remember specifically thinking, "This is strange. I never wake up like this." Now something you need to know about me is this girl *loves* her sleep. I cannot express that enough! Disturbances are not a welcome friend to me. If I am woken up, I am usually groggy and it takes a lot for me to fully wake. But this time it was different. This time I was alert.

Then, *almost* as if in an audible voice, but deep in my spirit, I heard God say, "I am healing your stomach." It was so clear and left no room in my mind for doubt. I was elated! But I also wanted to go back to sleep. I thought to myself, "Ok. Cool. Thanks God. You've got this. Wake me when you're done." And I partially fell asleep. There was complete confidence in my spirit that God would do what He said He would do, and I just needed to receive it (which is another great lesson about receiving from God rather than feeling we need to do something to get it).

For the next 15 minutes, I was not fully asleep but not fully awake; I was in a semi-sleep state. I remember that I was aware that God was healing me, and I felt this warm swishing, swirling feeling in my stomach. Then I would drift somewhat back to sleep. And then a few minutes later, the same would happen.

After about 15 minutes had passed, God woke me up again and said, "Your stomach is healed." And I felt one last warm, swirling sensation in my abdomen and that was it. There I was, lying in my bed at 3:15 am in the morning and thinking to myself, "God just healed my stomach. God just healed my stomach!! God JUST HEALED MY STOMACH! And nothing like how I thought it would happen." My husband happened to notice I was awake and he said, "Why are you up?"

"Something cool just happened but I can tell you in the morning," I whispered.

"Okay," he said, and turned back over to go to sleep.

I lay there for another 30 seconds and then I realized I would be foolish not to tell him, not to share this good news that I wanted to shout from the mountain tops! This was the healing we had been praying for for five years. This was BIG news! This was too big to contain…in fact I couldn't keep it in. Bursting with excitement I blurted out, "Wait…can I tell you now?"

"Okay," he said, still half asleep himself.

"God just healed my stomach," Waiting for an exuberance of excitement, I couldn't wait to hear what he'd say!

"Oh, that's great, hun," and he rolled back over and went back to sleep. Something else you should know? My husband likes his sleep, too.

With all that excitement pulsing through me, I have no idea how I was able to fall back asleep. When I woke up a few hours later, I almost couldn't believe what had happened. There were a few moments when I asked, "Did I just imagine that? Or dream it?" But I felt this deep and strong knowing inside of me that I cannot explain. I believe it was my spirit knowing the truth and trying to get my mind to comprehend it. I also kept reminding myself of Proverbs 3:5: "lean not on your own understanding." Some things we just have to trust without logic or reason and have faith in what God is doing!

Before that night, I had been struggling with ongoing stomach issues for half a decade. I had over twenty different foods I could not eat without quite intense stomach pain as well as some majorly prominent food groups, like gluten and dairy, which are in almost everything, that also caused pain. Even foods deemed to be safe would sometimes surprise me and cause me pain. I had been to doctors and specialists many, many times but all the while, I was praying for an answer and praying for healing. On a hike two years prior, I had sensed God say, "Be patient, your healing is coming." And so I continually held hope in my heart that I would be healed, never knowing how long it would take or in what way. Would it be miraculously or would it be through the medical system? I didn't know, but I held onto the faith to keep hoping for it.

Through reading some books on healing in the past, I learned the first thing you should do after receiving healing is to test it out. One of the things I hadn't been able to digest or eat without pain is eggs. I decided my first meal was going to be my favourite breakfast ever: over-easy eggs on a slice of warm, buttery toast. In fact, I did it up good: I made two!

Testing it out seems like it would be easy but oh boy, did it take faith. I had become so accustomed to eggs equaling pain that I still prepared myself for the consequences, all the while trusting in my heart that I had been healed.

I sat down, warm eggs and toast on the plate in front of me and I picked up my fork. As I sliced my knife through the bread and gooey egg, I didn't hesitate to immediately bring it up to my mouth to take my first bite. I savoured the taste of the warm yolk washing over my tongue and down my throat. The crispiness of the warm toast, soaked in creamy yolk as it rolled around my mouth was like heaven on earth. Five years…for five years I had dreamed about enjoying eggs again. And here I was, eating them like a champ!

I waited 20 minutes (historically, for me, that always seemed to be about when the stomach pain would ensue) and there was no pain at all! You know how you can sometimes feel two things at once? It was like one part of me was shocked and surprised that I was healed and that there was no pain, and the other part of me wasn't even phased because I knew in my heart that I had received a touch from God! We humans are funny creatures.

Thanking God, I truly felt so blessed. As you may know, it's kind of standard among Christians to pray for their food. Often it's a quick, 'Thank you Lord for this food. Please bless it our bodies. Amen." Before the prayer is even over, at least one person already has the fork ready to go. It can be so habitual that we forget what we are really saying. Well never have I ever prayed such a heartfelt prayer for my food before eating it than I did that day!

The next thing I did was even more risky. Dairy specifically was a huge trigger for pain. But I was determined in my heart that if God was going to be so good as to heal me, I was going to honour Him by stepping out. So I did what any logical person would do…I took the kids to Dairy Queen! And I ordered a small blizzard with all the 'fixins'. Ice-cream never tasted so good! Twenty minutes passed and again, no pain! I gave thanks to God and my faith increased!

To end off the last meal of the day, I decided I needed to step out and tackle the biggest giant of all, my nemesis for the last five years: gluten. It had wreaked havoc on my stomach for so many years that gluten and I weren't on speaking terms anymore. Gluten didn't like me and I didn't like it. We had resolved to 'agree to disagree.' But here I was, about to eat it and I knew and had confidence that I was going to be okay!

I took the first bite of the breaded chicken and decided I wasn't going to be afraid but I was going to walk out what God had done for me with confidence. One bite. Two bites. 10 bites later…no pain! I was elated. My family was elated! We all prayed and thanked God for His goodness to me!

That's a great story of healing and I love to share it. I share it as much as I can because testimony breeds faith. And I want to share the goodness of our God, and honour Him for what He's done. But that's not the end of the story. See, I think we hear these great stories of healing and we think it's like a fairytale ending that we are programmed to believe, "and they all lived happily ever after." And in many ways, that's true. It's one of the greatest blessings in my life to be able to eat food without fear. I am happy because it's changed my life in so many good ways.

But it's also been a journey from that day until now. There have been many times my faith has been tested to believe that God had healed me. There are times when I still have to step out in faith and push fear away in order to eat these foods that were once forbidden to me. There are still times when the enemy tries again, one more time to see if he can try to convince me that I'm not healed, that I should still be afraid of those foods. It doesn't happen every day, but it does happen, especially right when I was first healed.

I assumed that receiving healing would mean bliss from then on but I realized in the months following the healing, that God does the physical work and our job is to walk out the healing in faith. Our job is to believe that He is who He says He is. That He did what He said He did. To resist the devil's lies and continue to walk out our faith and trust in God.

> *God does the physical work and our job is to walk out the healing in faith.*

"Submit yourselves, then, to God. Resist the devil, and He will flee from you" James 4:7 (NIV).

Here is the part of the story that often gets missed in healing stories and I wanted to be clear about it, to remove the fairytale of it all and reveal the raw truth of the process of healing. There were times after my healing when I would doubt for a moment. It wasn't long but it was long enough, maybe a split second, maybe a few minutes, where I would doubt I had been healed. Or someone would ask me, "Are you sure you can have that?" "Are you sure it's good for you?" and I would question the validity of their query. I know it was the enemy trying to whisper doubt in my ear. But God has been faithful and keeps reminding me that I know what I heard and felt, and that the proof is in the fact that I can eat all these foods freely now. It's become so much easier to stand in that truth but I just want to encourage you that even in the healing, we still have to trust in God, maybe even more so than before the healing takes place.

Healing is a beautiful thing. It's changed my life. Travelling is easier. Dining with friends is easier. Backyard barbecues are easier. Life has become so much simpler. I am so grateful for the gift God has given me and I pray that you will have faith to believe for healing in your life, for whatever that need is. Whether it's physical, emotional, or situational. God wants to bind up our wounds and heal the broken hearted (Psalm 147:3) and we can call on Him, having faith and hope that He will come through.

But at the very same time, God knows the best timing. And that's why He waited until then. He knew that I needed faith to step out and walk this out. I know it's not a coincidence that the month before my stomach healing and leading up to it, I had been led to read the book *The Essential Guide to Healing*. It is a book written by two evangelical preachers (Bill Johnson and Randy Clark) about God's work healing people during healing and deliverance conferences around the world. The book tells great stories of incredible experiences of faith and healing, and how important it is to walk out those healings. God knew I needed to have my mind transformed just as much as my physical body and that book helped prepare my heart and mind, renewing my faith and tearing down paper-thin, former beliefs that I needed to reassess.

I had expected God to fit into my box when the healing came. Before the healing, when I would pray, I wanted to be sure I would know when He healed me and so in my prayers, I would suggest to God how He could let me know, or how He could go about it (it sounds so silly to say that out loud, now!). I would say things like, "And when/if you heal my stomach, please do it in an obvious way, so I'll know. Like, make it growl really loud or give me a dream about it, so I'll know." I always attached my one-dimensional plan to His artistry, not considering the fact that God knows *just* how to do it, *just* how to orchestrate it so I *would* know. In the beautiful way He so often chooses, He healed me in a wonderfully poetic and gentle way. Like a parent who nurses their child back to health when they're sick, bending down to their level at their bedside and wiping their forehead with a cool cloth. I could not deny the warm swirling in my stomach. I could not deny His voice. I could not deny the truth that was in my heart and spirit, even when I was tested so many times to doubt the validity of it all. Just like what Jesus says in John 10:27, "My sheep hear my voice, and I know them, and they follow me" (ESV). It's so true and that situation helped build my faith to hear God's voice in many other ways and decisions in my life.

Do you still think I'm selfish for asking for another healing? Do you think that asking for another healing means we can't appreciate and be thankful for what God has already done? I do believe we need to be ever grateful, deliberately thankful for God's blessings in our lives. Whether it's healing or some other beautiful gift, gratitude is so important. It changes mindsets and brain chemistry. It changes situations and outcomes. We can choose to be grateful in the midst of a trial, not just *after* the trial. I thank God so often for what He's done because I never want to take for granted what He did for me.

God invites us to rest in Him and also to ask of Him, however, I believe God knows our hearts and He will give His children what they need. That's a promise. If I continue to pray for my knee to be healed and it doesn't happen this side of heaven, I'm okay with that. But if I don't pray for it at all, I am not following the example in the Word. God says we need to ask (Matthew 7:7), and so I will be diligent in doing my part and let God be in charge of His part. I can't do His part, only He can. And He won't do my part, only I can. Together, this is how we co-labour with God.

I am grateful for my stomach healing. I am also thankful that God heard my prayer and answered it. I will never know if God would have healed me if I hadn't prayed for it. I don't try to understand all those details; those are His to design. But I do know, that of all the examples we are given in Scripture, the people who received healing were the ones who asked (Luke 8:40-48, John 11, John 5, are a few examples). Look these stories up. Read them. Meditate on them. See what God has done.

I will be obedient to what He says in His Word and let Him be my guide, daily being grateful for what He has already done.

Like Paul says in Philippians 4:6, we present our requests before God *with* thanksgiving. We want to honour God for what He has done and is doing, rather than complaining about what we don't have. We don't want to become entitled children. Entitled children need firm boundaries and consistency to learn self-control. And entitlement can happen slowly and easily. We can feel entitled or owed when we go through hardships, or when we pray for something and don't see (in our limited understanding or with our human eyes) God answering that prayer. You do have a choice though: allow a root of bitterness to enter your soul or trust that

God is good and is at work, regardless of how obvious or unseen it may be. The latter? That's faith. That is the conviction of things hoped for and the evidence of things unseen (Hebrews 11:1). The choice is yours.

What Does This Have to Do with God's Care for Us?

Without doing a 'heart check-in' with yourself, it's easy for a root of bitterness to grow in your heart after enduring a hardship; it's human nature, but it's also an easy entry point for Satan. Like I said earlier, bitterness is slow and sneaky and we have to be on alert for it. Pray about it. Talk to God about it. Be sure that you're honest with yourself and God, and let Him come in and be your Healer. That's one of the single-most important things you can do.

Adding to that, before I was healed, I walked the long road of struggle, too. I spent many visits travelling to new cities, to meet new doctors in hopes of finding a solution, huddled over in pain at the hospital. I spent days in pain with a stomach that wouldn't tolerate anything but water sometimes. I was poked and prodded by doctors, naturopaths, specialists, nurse practitioners…all trying to find out what was wrong with my stomach. I spent five years enduring what can only be described as ongoing pain from food. The reality is that eating isn't optional, it's vital; so, eating resulting in pain was unavoidable. Only someone who's gone through it can understand the frustration, and the same is true with your story. Only you, or someone who's gone through a similar situation to you, can understand your story, your journey, your pain. It's hard and messy, and it's riddled with all kinds of pain and hardship. Only God really knows the tears you've cried over it, the pain you've endured, the thoughts that keep you awake. But even in the midst of that, God *is* there and He *does* care.

In that sense, I do know what you're going through. I know that you feel like you're not sure you can hold on when you're hurting so badly. I know many days you feel you are white-knuckled, holding onto your faith. I know you feel like if you could just receive healing, you would never ask for anything else again. I know you may feel like the only way you can know God cares is for Him to remove this burden from you. Even Jesus—perfect Jesus—asked God to remove the burden from Him.

> "Father, if you are willing, **take this cup from me**; yet not my will, but yours be done" Luke 22:42 (NIV, emphasis mine).

It's okay. You can be honest with God; Jesus was. This verse also should remind you that Jesus, in all His perfection, also asked for the burden of death on a cross to be removed; so much so that He sweat blood. He felt it all. He understands *your* pain. He knows what you're going through. And He catches all your tears and places them in a bottle (Psalm 56:8). Think about that. When you're crying, He's there, not letting one tear fall that is unaccounted for. He holds you close in the midst of it all.

If God took Jesus's suffering away, His plan wouldn't have been accomplished. We would still be under the old law given to the

Israelites and our lives would be so different. Instead, God gave Jesus the ability to go through it. He gave Him the strength He needed.

Even though we are not given as monumental a task as Jesus—to be the Saviour of the world—God sees our struggle and He gives us the grace and ability to handle it under pressure. He supplies what we need in order to come through it, victorious, even if it doesn't feel like it sometimes. That's where we have to stop being led by our feelings and instead trust in God that He *is* giving us what we need. We need to believe the promises of God more than we believe our feelings. Feelings can mislead us and don't always accurately portray the truth, but the Word of God is truth. We can always rely on it.

I love what it says in Hebrews 12:4: "In your struggle against sin, you have not yet resisted to the point of shedding your blood." Jesus is so closely acquainted with our suffering. He doesn't look at us and say, "Oh yeah, that must be hard but good luck with it all. I'll try to get to it soon." He doesn't sit on His throne in heaven and tally up our right from our wrong, to see which way the scale tips in order to decide if He will help us. He doesn't compare us with someone else in need and choose to help the one with more gold stars. He doesn't look at our pain from a distance; it says in Psalm 139:3 that He is "intimately acquainted" with all your ways. He feels what we feel.

God sent Jesus here to be *fully* man and *fully* God so that He could be acquainted with our pain and suffering. He knows firsthand what it feels like to suffer and be a human being. He has so much compassion for you. He wants you to know that He is right there in the mud with you. Just like He was in the fire with Shadrach, Meshach and Abednego, He also knows when and how to deliver you, and as hard as it is, we need to trust His timing. He will never allow more to come on us than we can bear, and He will provide the way out. The hard part is often in the waiting.

> "And let us run with perseverance the race marked out for us, fixing our eyes on Jesus, the pioneer and perfecter of faith. For the joy set before Him **He endured the cross**, scorning its shame, and sat down at the right hand of the throne of God. **Consider Him who endured such opposition from sinners, so that you will not grow weary and lose heart**" (Hebrews 12:4 NIV, emphasis mine).

It seems that it is in the waiting period when those doubts creep in. That's when you hear whispers from the enemy that maybe God has forgotten about you, or maybe He's too busy for you; maybe you haven't done enough to earn healing, or earn your way out of the problem. Perhaps you wonder if God is angry with you for the things you've done in the past. That maybe you are being taught a lesson or being punished. To seal the deal, he whispers his most poisonous statement of all, "If God really loved you, He'd take this suffering away."

He doesn't have to be blatantly obvious in his lies; he says just enough to place doubt in your mind, to shake your faith in questioning God's care for you or God's love for you because the enemy knows that God's love for us is one of the most life-changing things to us and one of the most dangerous things to the enemy. The enemy knows that if we truly and fully understood God's love, nothing could separate us from all the faith and all the hope and all the trust available.

> "For I am convinced that neither death nor life, neither angels nor demons, neither the present nor the future, nor any powers, neither height nor depth, nor anything else in all creation, will be able to separate us from the love of God that is in Christ Jesus our Lord" Romans 8:38-39 (NIV)

I spent many days, months and years waiting for healing. I have spent many days, months and years waiting for other things that have not yet come to pass in my life. But I still have faith for those things! It is easy to begin to feel impatient or to feel like you're losing hope, but those are the times when you have to step out even further in faith, building yourself up in the Word and in prayer, trusting in God—even if you're white-knuckled while doing it!

> "Blessed is a man who perseveres under trial; for once He has been approved, He will receive the crown of life which the Lord has promised to those who love Him," (James 1:12, NIV).

It reminds me of the story of Lazarus as told in John 11:1-45. Lazarus' sisters, Mary and Martha, had asked Jesus to come heal their brother because He was dying. Lazarus was also a friend of

Jesus. Had I been present there, I would have expected Jesus to drop what He was doing and head right over to see Lazarus. But He didn't. He was never rushed. Do you notice that about Jesus? He doesn't conform to the busy, rushed mentality that the rest of us do. I believe it's because He not only knows what the outcome will be but also because He wants to wait a bit, and grow our faith…to see if we really trust Him.

Jesus tells them, "This sickness will not end in death" (John 11:4).

As they're waiting for Jesus, Lazarus dies. Not only is he dead, but he's been dead for four days by the time Jesus arrives. I can imagine in the humid and hot temperatures of the Middle East, he was beginning to smell; in fact, it was so strong that John mentioned that detail in his writing of the gospel.

What was the family thinking at this time? Were they still hopeful? It must have been confusing for them. It may have looked like Jesus was wrong in telling them that the sickness wasn't going to end in death, because it looked like it did. I can imagine they would have had some doubts. But I believe that when Jesus said it would not end in death, He was speaking about the entire story, not just the immediate. He knew that in the end, Lazarus would be healed and live.

Four days later, Jesus showed up, as if right on schedule. No crowds. Just Jesus. When He came to the tomb, it says that He wept. I find it beautiful that the scriptures record this. It may seem like a tiny detail to some, yet I see this detail as one that so clearly shows the Saviour's heart, the compassion He feels for His people,

His friends, His beloved. He understands feelings and emotions. He feels them, too, and I believe this detail shows that Jesus, too, felt the pain of death, the heartache of Mary and Martha and that He, too, was aquatinted with their pain.

Shortly after, He tells them to open the tomb and He calls out to Lazarus to get up and walk, and to leave his grave clothes behind. I think that's significant. Leaving behind the things of old, the things that aren't relevant anymore, the things of our former lives. He immediately heals Lazarus and everyone goes on their way. Imagine what it must have been like to not only see this miracle occur, but to *be* Lazarus, who died and was then resurrected?

The message I take from this is that Jesus wasn't concerned about the timing. He wasn't rushed. **He knew that His abilities were not limited by time or space.** And the same is true today because Jesus hasn't changed. We see things in the finite, in the 'here and now' but Jesus does not. He knows the end of the story. He knows what He can do. He knows that God will take care of us. And it seems that our only job is to trust Him. To trust Him that He *will* deliver us at the ***appointed*** time. It may have appeared to Mary and Martha that all hope was lost—it doesn't say—but even still, Jesus showed up and delivered Lazarus just as He said He would.

CHAPTER 8

Authenticity and Transparency in Struggle

One of the single most important things we can do for ourselves and for others is to be authentic. Being authentic with ourselves, being authentic with our own feelings and being aware of how we feel and dealing with our emotions or struggles is paramount in growing as humans but also growing in our relationship with God. We cannot grow or change or be salt and light when we are bound to the hangups we face. There are so many things that shape who we are and many of them are good but there are some that shape us negatively. Those are the areas where God wants to step in and shed light so we can recognize the cycle of hurt or pain or bad habits, so He can show us the way out of this pattern. If we don't check in with our feelings, actions, priorities and perspectives, we can lose sight of what we are doing. How do you become authentic with yourself? I'm so glad you asked.

First of all, being authentic with yourself starts not with yourself, but with God. David prayed, "Search me, God, and know my heart; test me and know my anxious thoughts. See if there is any offensive way in me, and lead me in the way everlasting" Psalm 139:24 (NIV). This should also be our daily prayer. We can be stubborn and we often don't see our own faults. We make all kinds of excuses as to why we are the way we are and we are quick to notice someone else stepping out of place, but are incredibly forgiving to our own behaviour.

We lose out on what God has for us when we don't ask Him to search our hearts. As it says in Matthew 7:3, "And why worry about a speck in your friend's eye when you have a log in your own?" Part of our nature is to see the fault in someone else and not in ourselves. This is why it's so important to ask *God* to show you what He wants to show you. Listen to His voice. Sit and be quiet with Him and see what comes to your mind. And don't just do it once a year. Make this a regular habit in your life. I know for me it's become a part of my daily walk. While it doesn't mean I behave properly all the time, I do notice that when I pray this, God often brings situations or things to my mind that I need to work on or ask for guidance on. But He's so gentle. And often times, He has been preparing my heart beforehand so that I'm ready to receive what He has to say.

Another way God speaks this to us in our lives is through repetitive themes. What I mean by this is sometimes a situation will occur over and over and it can be God's gentle way of showing you that it's something He wants you to pray about. Pay attention to repetitive situations or themes in your life. It may be God prompting you to work on something. God always starts off gently, wanting you to take notice but if you don't pay attention to His prompting, and you keep ignoring it, He will often use more drastic and obvious ways. Take the time to pray daily for God to show you what He wants you to change or grow in, and see what He impresses upon your heart. Even if it's something hard and something you don't want to deal with, follow the prompting of the Holy Spirit to take the first step, knowing that God will show you what to do and that He will work on your heart, day by day.

Think of it like a a bullet wound. The bullet represents some issue you have or something that God wants to change in you (a bad attitude, a hard time being kind to people, etc). When the bullet is embedded in your skin, infection can start to take place. The longer it stays in, the more the infection can grow because there's something foreign in there that is impeding the healthy tissue to heal. As time progresses, the wound can become so infected and full of gangrene that it can start to affect other parts of the body. It can become poisonous to the rest of the body and even lead to death. In the same way, there are bullets (areas we need help in, sin in our lives, attitudes or problems we need to deal with) that can cause infection in our lives if left untreated. God sees those bullets in us and He wants to remove them so that they don't cause infection in our lives and so He can heal the wound. We are often less likely to see the bullets ourselves, and we need to let God come in and show us where they are, let Him remove them (as we co-labour with Him) and as a result, let Him heal us. Yes, we have a part in that as He shows and leads us in what to do, but He is our Physician and we need to let Him show us so we can submit to Him removing the bullet and then begin to heal. It's a beautiful, loving, caring thing that God wants to heal us, but sometimes it's hard to receive the correction that comes beforehand. However, we cannot move onto the healing in our lives without first having the bullet removed (the correction). I really encourage you to be open to being authentic and transparent with yourself, and God, by letting Him show you what you need to work on. He already knows, He's just waiting for you to receive what He has to say so He can begin the surgeon's work of removing it.

The other important component of authenticity is to be authentic with those in our circle, to be authentic in who we are, in how we use our words, how we share our struggles, our plans, our victories. Being real is the best gift you can give someone and it's part of living a life of truth. Now being real doesn't mean we dump all our stuff on others but it does mean we don't subscribe to the 'pretend reality' that so many do. It leads to a very distorted 'reality' online and some people have a hard time recognizing that what they are seeing online is not, in fact, reality. It's an edited version of life. Being authentic is about being who you say you are and living that out. It's about being the same way to someone's face as you are when they're not around. It's about the small things that no one else sees but that you do because you know it's right and that it honours God.

Being authentic and transparent doesn't mean we dump all our issues on our circle of friends, either, and load them up with all our problems. We can lovingly ask for prayer when we feel the need to share a struggle while also being mindful that God should be the first one we go to.

There is a difference between being authentic and being ostentatious or arrogant with our views. There is a growing attitude in our word that says, "Well that's just me, so DEAL!" There is an attitude of entitlement to act however they want to act, with no accountability to God or any accountability to be kind. That is hardly the exemplary behaviour of a follower of Christ whose heart is open to God's chastisement and change. I'm sure you, too, have encountered this many times in your life and agree that it really doesn't exemplify the heart or life of Christ. We should be asking for chastisement and correction not only so we can be better and a better witness, but also because God's chastisement is only to shed light on the dark places and bring healing and restoration. Authenticity doesn't mean we are garish and push things in others' faces; but it means that we are real about who we are, what we are facing and live the same way around others as we are in our thought life. Believe me, I'm speaking to myself here, too. I need these same reminders.

Authenticity and being open has the ability to open doors, and transform our lives, and the lives of those around us. When we allow God to change and mould us, we can also be open to those around us about what God is doing inside of us. This can propel even greater changes in us and be a source of encouragement to others in their journeys.

Authenticity and Transparency with God

Authenticity and transparency is about being real and true to those around you—yes—but the other side of those two things is being authentic and transparent with God. You may be asking what I am talking about. You may be saying to yourself, *Of course I am real with God. He knows my thoughts and feelings even before I do.* That is true, but are you being honest with God about the questions you have or the things on your mind that you feel are too taboo to even say out loud? I know I have struggled with that. In fact, when I was praying about what to title this book, it immediately came to me (I believe it was put on my heart by the Holy Spirit) but I really wrestled with it for months. Why? Because I felt that it was such a jarring question. I felt that I would be judged because this question could seem irreverent; that this is not a question we would dare ask God. This question is taboo, nothing that anyone would ask out loud or be honest with a friend about. I knew that it would rub some the wrong way or stop people in their tracks, and make them pause. But, I also knew it was a question that needed an answer because it was being asked by the world; pre-Covid19 and post-Covid19. This question is crying out of humanity's souls, especially during this time of a global pandemic, but this question is not isolated to this time—it has been around for thousands of years.

After I had prayed about it and wrestled with it, I knew that this was what God was calling me to title the book. The fact that it is such a taboo question will hopefully cause people to stop and search their heart. And I think it's so incredibly important to be real and honest with the things we wrestle with rather than keep them cooped up on the inside of us. Keeping our feelings cooped up and stuffed down is one the worst things we can do for ourselves emotionally but also physically and spiritually.

God already knows your thoughts anyway—it says so in Psalm 139:1-3, "Lord you have examined me and know all about me. You know when I sit down and when I get up. You know my thoughts before I think them. You know where I go and where I lie down. You know everything I do. Lord, even before I say a word, you already know it" (NCV). If He already knows your thoughts, then why are you afraid to say it out loud? Do you think that you're hiding your feelings from Him? God is not mad at you if you have questions. He knows them anyway, so why do we have such a hang-up about saying them out loud?

I believe it stems from a few things. First off, I want to say that the following scenarios I am speaking about are regarding those in particular who are Christ followers. There are of course those who don't believe in God or they do believe in Him but don't have a relationship with Him, or are angry at God. This last group has been asking this question for a long time and are typically not as shy at talking about it. They are at least honest with their questions and feelings about God. But that is not who I'm specifically speaking about here. I am speaking about Christ-followers, Christians. I think we need to be honest with the fact that as Christ-followers we need to start talking about the things that we think we shouldn't talk about.

As I said before, I believe there are a few factors as to why we, as Christians, are afraid to be honest about our concerns or questions with God. The first group are those who were raised to believe that God is waiting to catch you messing up. They grow up with a vague worry about making mistakes or displeasing God. They feel that they have to do everything right and then God will be pleased with them. The second group believes that wondering this question isn't wrong but saying it out loud is. They think that saying it out loud makes it sinful or they think that if they don't say it out loud, the thought will just go away (just to let you know, even thoughts you try to 'stuff' down don't ever go away so this just compounds the issue bothering you). Third, there's a group of people who think these kinds of questions are so taboo and wrong that to even utter them would ostracize them from their friends or community.

Here's the thing: all three of those reasons don't change the fact that these questions do arise from time to time our minds, even though they might not be 'good' questions or the right question, or they might be questions founded in fear or doubt or worry, they are still questions that are on our minds. We cannot ignore the question just because it doesn't fit into a box. We can't be afraid to be transparent with God. We cannot be avoidant of our feelings and queries because avoiding them doesn't make them go away.

Added to that, all of those reasons why people avoid being transparent with their questions to God are rooted in fear. Fear of God being angry with them, fear of being honest with themselves and God and fear of others' opinions. Fear is a crazy little beast that wedges its way into our minds and makes us believe lies. Satan, our enemy, is the father of lies. He is more than happy to try to convince us that any of those three arguments are true. He doesn't want you to have a close relationship with God. He wants you to live in fear.

But look at King David. If you read through the Psalms, you can see that David wrestled with some very big issues. He wasn't afraid to be honest and ask God questions that were 'taboo.' He was very open with God about questions he had or how he felt. And yet, God said that David was a 'man after his own heart' (1 Samuel 13:14). God didn't punish David for bringing questions to Him. He loved David and He wanted to give him the answers he sought.

We aren't doing God any 'favours' by keeping our questions to ourselves. I mean, yes, of course it would be lovely to go through life, having it all figured out and never doubt one moment or have any questions about anything. But that's not at all the way life works. This is an unrealistic expectation and it's not one that God has for us. Many times in Scripture we hear Jesus saying, "Ask." My two favourite verses about this are Matthew 7:7, "Ask, and it will be given to you; seek, and you will find; knock, and it will be opened to you," and Jeremiah 29:13, "You will seek me and find me when you seek me with all your heart." It's so clear that *God is not afraid of your hard questions*. He welcomes them! He wants us to come to Him and be transparent with our feelings. As I said before, He knows them anyway. Who are we trying to protect? Are you worried you'll hurt God's feelings if you ask Him the questions that are burning in your heart? God would rather you come to Him with your questions than stuff them inside and wrestle with them on your own.

In these kinds of scenarios, I think about my relationship with my own children. As my kids have grown up, there have been times when they've needed to ask questions to learn things. Things like, "How do I ride a bike?" or "How does a chicken lay eggs?" Those are simple questions they would ask when they were younger but as they grow older, they have more complicated questions. Questions about life or about relationships. Questions about God. And I cannot tell you how blessed I am that my children feel comfortable enough to ask me about these things. It truly honours me. I love that they want to seek counsel or want to honour us as parents. It blesses and encourages me that they want to know things from their parents. The truth is that I know their heart is pure in seeking our words and wisdom. I don't get offended when they ask me the hard questions. Instead, I am able to reassure them in whatever way they need. I don't expect my children to know everything and I would rather be the one to tell them what they seek to know than for someone else tell them.

I truly believe and I see evidence in Scripture that God feels the same way about us when we are wrestling with questions. Even if the questions are hard and taboo. Even if they're raw, real and seem hurtful to you, God knows your wonderings anyway, and He wants to be the first one to answer them. He doesn't want the enemy sneaking in ideas or a friend putting a wrong thought in your mind. Those things can easily happen but if we are going to the Source, the Truth and the Life, we can't go wrong. We honour God by being transparent with Him in our prayers. Asking God the questions you wrestle with isn't wrong or sinful.

David asked God plenty of hard questions like, "Will you forget me forever?" (Psalm 31:1) and, "My God, my God, why have you forsaken me?" (Psalm 22:1). David wasn't afraid to ask the hard questions and you shouldn't be either.

When I realized that I had been wrestling with the question of God's care for me, I knew that it had been a question I was struggling with for months but was too afraid to ask. It was bottled up inside of me, like a can of pop that's been shaken up. It took time for me to be honest with myself and with God about what I was feeling but once I did, I surrendered it to God and He came in and spoke truth to me, and I felt peace wash over me. I realized that I needed to learn more about who God is and revisit some thoughts that had been subconsciously rattling around in my mind. We need to stop being afraid of being honest and realize that God is not mad at us. We need to be able to be okay with being honest with ourselves and with God without feeling guilt or shame. We need to bring our thoughts, concerns and questions to God so that He can begin to answer them for us and let the truth set us free (John 8:32).

CHAPTER 9

I'm in the Middle of It, Now What?

When you're in the middle of the storm is when you're tempted the most by the enemy. He knows your weak moments and he wants to use every opportunity to destroy your faith and your relationship with God. **Thankfully,** nothing can separate us from the love of God (Romans 8:38-39). God is always there with us, helping us and speaking to us. Nothing can separate us—ever.

We can make choices though, of our own volition, that distance us from God, such as being angry or bitter towards the situation. And believe me, I know it's easy to be angry when you're in pain. I know it's easy to be frustrated, bitter, sad—all the range of emotions one can feel when you're in the midst of the storm. That's perhaps *not* the easiest time to raise your hands and praise God. It can feel nearly impossible to lift your hands in harmonious worship to God. You may love Him, but when you're in the storm, finding the words to praise Him is the hardest. Yet may I tell you the truth? Even if it's not what you want to hear and even if you don't want to do it? That is the *most* important time to do it. When it's the hardest to do it, open your mouth and thank God for what He is doing. Open Psalms and sing a song of praise to God, or speak it over yourself, even if you can only say it with a whisper.

See, when you open your mouth and praise God, it may take a little time for your heart to catch up to your spirit but it will get there. Your spirit already praises God within you, and the Holy Spirit lives inside of you and helps guide you to praise. When you go against what feels easy and agree with the Holy Spirit, you are doing warfare against the enemy. Satan doesn't want to see you victorious. He wants to see you defeated and angry, bitter. When the enemy sees you bitter he thinks he is winning because a bitter person is not a happy or joyful person exuding Jesus' love.

What does bitterness do? Does it add any joy to your life or does it just rob you of your peace and happiness? Even though it is hard to praise at first, your spirit will agree with you and that practice will turn into authentic praise. The traps the enemy has set for you to fall into (anger, bitterness) will be defeated because you are resisting him. Praise opens the door for God to fling wide the gates of heaven and show the enemy that he is defeated. You are reminding the enemy that you are a child of God and that nothing can separate you from God. Just like when Jesus was tempted in the desert, He defeated the enemy by speaking the truth of the Word, and it says in Luke 4:13 that the enemy, having been defeated, went away and waited for a more opportune time. The enemy knows that praise is the antidote to suffering. Praise is the cure for the brokenhearted. Even though it feels like the opposite of what you may want to do, I implore you: *do it*. Muster up all the energy you have and praise Him. Even if it's by reading through the Psalms and whispering them to yourself. Even it's a short and simple prayer of gratitude. Even if it's a slow start, I *promise* you that it will change the atmosphere and will let the enemy know whose you are and who your faith and trust is in. Not to mention it reminds *you* who your faith and trust are in. It will begin to flow out of you and you'll see your heart change.

We cannot control our circumstances (trust me, you may think you can but you cannot- save yourself the stress!) but we can control how we react to them. We can control how we behave when we are in the middle of the storm. How we react to our circumstances has a large part to do with our faith. When Jesus was praying in the garden of Gethsemane, right in the middle of the battle, preparing for the incredible sacrifice He was going to make —even though He asked God to take the cup from Him if it be His will—He still committed to go through it. He still trusted God to bring Him through it. He *knew* the terribly difficult sacrifice He was going to go through and *still*, in the middle of it, when He could have turned away, He stepped forward. He trusted God to bring Him through. He stepped out in faith.

That's the Saviour of the world though, you might argue. *He's the Son of God. He had divine ability to endure it.* Yes, He did. I agree. But He was *fully* man and fully God. He was scared to the point of sweating blood, demonstrating His full humanity, His very real humanness. Even when He hung on the cross, He said, "My God, my God, why have you forsaken me?" He was honest about what He was going through, His emotions and feelings. He was human and had real emotions, real questions, perhaps—arguably—real doubts in that moment.

I want to make a point here. Jesus, too, had a moment of questioning God, asking why. He loved God, He trusted Him, He was willing to *die* for Him and for us, yet even Jesus—the perfect Son of God—had a moment of questioning. I am not saying this to justify always questioning God. In a perfect world we would never question Him, we would just trust Him. *But,* I will also say that we are human and in our humanness, there is a quest to question things from time to time, even if we do trust in God and even if we are willing to do what God asks us. To expect us to be perfect is impossible. To suggest that for the rest of your life you will never have a moment of questioning or doubt would be nice but it's unrealistic. Be real, open and honest with God. *But don't let that be the place you park your heart.*

Jesus loved His Father. Yet, in the middle of the struggle, He had a moment of questioning. I emphasize this because I want to give you a moment to recognize that you may question things sometimes. You have to be honest with what you're feeling, otherwise you're setting yourself up for unresolved feelings, and that's where bitterness and anger can take root.

It's okay to want the suffering to stop. But in those moments, cry out to **G.O.D.** Not to your friend or on social media. Call out to Him, as Jesus did when He hung on the cross. Be open with Him; He knows your thoughts before you even think them and He loves you anyway! Your feelings don't change His love for you. Your pain and questioning don't make Him love you any more or any less. Nothing you do can change His love for you or His care for you.

David frequently cried out to God. Sometimes when I read the Psalms I feel like I'm reading the letter of two different men—one who trusts God and the other who questions God's plans in his life. He just cannot make up his mind on what he feels. But are we any different? We sometimes struggle to find the words to express ourselves or we bounce around from mountains to valleys like a pinball machine. In an instant we can change our mindset or our feelings. We can be distraught and down trodden in one moment but then we get a word from God or a verse that speaks to us and moments later our faith is renewed.

Keep looking for God! Don't become complacent and think you have to keep wandering around the wilderness without direction. He *is* guiding you. He *is* leading you. Keep looking for Him. Listen to Him. "My sheep listen to my voice; I know them, and they follow me" (John 10:27, NIV).

The Israelites took 40 years to make an 11 day journey. 11 days—that's how many days it would have taken had they gone straight through; instead, because they kept wandering around, it took them 40 years to make that journey. They had so many good things waiting for them, a land where crops grew easily (in those times that was very important), a place they would be free and not be enslaved, as well as so many other blessings God had planned for them. But rather than stepping into what God had for them, they spent 40 years wandering around the desert, not enjoying all that God had for them and grumbling the whole way through. God wanted better for them! And He wants better for you. How much do we miss out on because we get in our own way and we blame God, yet that's not His plan for us? His plans are so much better than what we walk into but sometimes we don't get there because we keep getting in our own way.

I'm going to give you an example of a woman that is not a real person, but an example of the Israelite 'wilderness mentality' that we often see exhibited in those around us and I share it with you to exemplify how we, as followers, can come alongside and support those around us who are struggling. I have seen this pattern many times in the world around me but I do believe there is an opportunity for helping create change.

Gennie was raised in church. She didn't have the best upbringing, her parents weren't exactly very nurturing and they fought a lot, among other things. Their parenting was misdirected and there were very few rules in her life. This led to a very confused, angry, and frustrated teenager, who grew into a very confused, angry and frustrated adult. She married, had one child and was not very happy. She struggled a lot to feel accepted and in not knowing how to function in life, had a lot of self-sabotaging behaviour. Some tragedies took place in her life that caused some very deep wounds.

At various times when these tragedies occurred, she would come to the end of herself, cling to Jesus and make Him the centre of her life for a while. She would attend church and prayer groups. She aimed to stop sinful behaviour and purify her heart and her life before God. It was as if God was her air and He became her lifeline in order to cope. Soon, through God's healing power and help, the pain of the tragedy would pass, she would heal from the pain and life would resume as normal for her.

Yet once life's pain had healed and life resumed normally for her, she ignored God and discounted what He had brought her through. She went back to living her life the way she wanted to, again. She would stop attending church, stop devoting time with God and she would put God on the back burner of her life. She went back to the sinful ways she was accustomed to. She sort of 'left Jesus behind' and went on with her life, without keeping Jesus at the centre. It's as if she would crash and burn, but when the scars had healed, she would return to the same life that led her to destruction. No matter how many times God delivered her, no matter how many amazing encounters she would have with Him, she would not keep Him at the centre of her life. She ultimately felt she had things under control, going her way and she wasn't about to let God tell her what to do. It's as if she turned from all that was good and all God had done for her, and decided she would still do things her way going forward, even though she'd seen it lead her to destruction.

Through this process, I have learned something about my role as a friend and helper. My job is not to do God's job. My job is not to make those who are struggling, do what I think they should do. My job is to love them through it. It's to be the hands and feet of Jesus, to forgive and move forward with supporting them in love and praying for them. It's to keep being an example that points them to Jesus. I cannot do God's job but I can be obedient to what God is asking me to do. I am not the antidote, God is. I am not perfect, God is. If He leads me, I will do what He asks but most of the time He's asking me to just love them through it, be there for them, and pray, pray, pray.

As the Holy Spirit has been speaking to me about this, the other thing I've come to realize is that we all have some of this human nature in us, this 'wilderness mentality'. Some appear to have it more than others but it's the same kind of story as the one of the Israelites. They prayed for freedom, they called out to God when they needed something and then when they got delivered from it and had experienced the victory, they would go back to their old way of doing things. How often do we follow the same pattern in our lives?

I believe God has changed that 'wilderness mentality' in me over the years as I've prayed about it, recognized it and asked God to change it in me, but I still the need to be watchful of my human nature tendency, realizing that it can rise back up if I let it. I have not yet become an expert at it. I still can fall back into it when I'm not being watchful. "Be alert and of sober mind. Your enemy the devil prowls around like a roaring lion looking for someone to devour. Resist Him, standing firm in the faith, because you know that the family of believers throughout the world is undergoing the same kind of sufferings" 1 Peter 5:8 (NIV).

In the story of the Israelites, they would find themselves in a terrible predicament such as lacking food or water, and they would cry out to Moses to ask God to help them. In God's mercy, He would! He would provide water out of a rock or feed them with manna from the sky (Exodus 16:4). He did it in His great mercy and He did it simply because He loved them and promised to take care of them.

Furthermore, He had so much waiting for them in the Promised Land. There were so many good things coming to them that He had planned for all 600,000 men (plus all the women and children) who were delivered from slavery. Of all of those 600,000 plus, first-generation Israelites delivered from slavery, only *two* of them—Joshua and Caleb—made it to the Promised Land. The children and grandchildren of those first-generation Israelites later made it to the Promised Land but of the original Israelites who were freed from slavery, only two made it. God had *planned* it for all of them, yet because they kept getting in their own way, complaining and turning back to sinful idols, they never got to fulfill or live out any of the promises and blessings God had for them. That is sad—how much more God had in store for them had they just followed what He asked of them.

As God revealed that to me, I began contemplating about how we live now. We often use or hear the story of the Israelites in the wilderness as a cautionary tale. We perhaps unknowingly judge them and think about what fools they were. We sit on our high horse at times, proudly thinking we would *never* be so foolish or sinful. We read all about what God did for them and we think, "How could they be so ungrateful? He provided all of their needs miraculously and yet, they still went back to their old ways! How *could* they?" However, before you get back up there on your high horse, stop for a moment and think about it. Are we really so different? God has provided all our needs, too. He has created miracles in our lives (whether you realize it or not) and He has good plans for us; He says so in His Word. Yet, still, we complain and grumble. We look at one tiny pebble in the road and we focus on that rather than the 100 mile straight stretch of road without so much as a fleck of dust on it. We take our eyes off of Jesus (the beautifully paved highway) and we focus only on the tiny pebble on the road (our problem).

That is exactly what the Israelites did. They forgot all that God did for them and they instead went back to their old ways (worshipping idols and sinful behaviour) and in doing so, they missed out on all the ***good*** plans God had for them.

Let me encourage you today that you don't have to make the same mistakes the Israelites did. He wants you to walk into the promised land of freedom, whatever that may be. Financial freedom, or victory over emotional or mental battles, or freedom from health struggles, or relationships restored and healed…God will fill in the blank! He has such good plans for you in your present and your future if you'll submit to *His will* and *His ways.* As recorded in John 5:30, Jesus said, "I can do nothing on My own initiative. As I hear, I judge; and My judgment is just, because I do not seek My own will, but the will of Him who sent Me." As Christ is our example, we should pray for the same attitude.

He's got the path paved for you; your job is to walk it out but if you keep getting tripped up on the tiny pebble in front of you, you'll miss out on all the goodness that's ahead.

I want to encourage you to instead keep your eyes on Jesus; He's your solution! He's got a plan worked out for your good and He wants to guide you into that. Don't spend 40 years making an 11 day journey. Don't wander around the wilderness; choose now to step into the promised land God has for you.

Resiliency

One thing that I've learned as I've gone through struggle after struggle is this: I am stronger than I realize. I am stronger than I give myself credit for. Not, however, for the reasons you might think. Not because of my own personal strength, but because Jesus is my strength when I am weak. When I feel exhausted, like I can't pick myself back up one more time, God reveals Himself and gives me the strength. When it seems like this is never going to end, God makes himself known and whispers in my ear, 'You've got one more fight inside."

Why does He say "one more", when realistically there's probably one-thousand more? Because God gives us strength for *today*. He promises the strength for each day and tells us not to worry about tomorrow's strength because it will be supplied when tomorrow comes. What a blessing to not to worry about the future or even the next day because we can rest in His promise that He will give us what we need to endure it! He gives us the "measure of faith" (Romans 12:3, ESV), for what we need to endure right now.

When I finally grasped that concept in Matthew 6:34, it set me free: "Give your entire attention to what God is doing right now, and don't get worked up about what may or may not happen tomorrow. God will help you deal with whatever hard things come up when the time comes" (MSG). No longer did I need to fret about my future struggles. No longer did I need to worry about that appointment I didn't want to have in two weeks. No longer do I need to fret about even what will happen tomorrow. I just need to focus on today—what God has called me to for today and what His plans for me are, *today*. Tomorrow, God will give me the strength to endure whatever comes…tomorrow. I can be secure in my strength for today in *Him*, and wait for a whole new batch of strength, tomorrow.

He promises the strength for each day and tells us not to worry about tomorrow's strength because it will be supplied when tomorrow comes.

What a blessing to know that each day we are given what we need to flourish. God is not skimpy in provision! I don't ever have to wonder, 'Will I be able to get through this?' because God says in His word that I will (2 Corinthians 12:9). And He always keeps His promises. In moments when I've felt like the next step is too hard, His amazing grace (no wonder a timeless song was written about it!) shows up and gives me that super-boost I need to keep going.

Don't think about *all* the struggles you may have ahead. That's going to bring anyone down if they are thinking about such negative things. It's a waste of time and it causes you stress, anxiety and worry. Instead, focus on today, what is in front of you today and trust that whatever that is, God will help you. Why can you trust that? Because it's a promise of His, written in His word. You can choose to believe your fickle feelings, or you can choose to believe God's Word. Which one will you choose? Your peace depends on it.

When I look at all that I've had to overcome, thankfully with the help of God, Jesus and the Holy Spirit, I have been able to come across to the other side in victory. I look back at all the hardships God has given me strength to endure and the trials He has spared me from and I can't do anything but be thankful. I wake up each morning desiring and planning to not mess up but daily, I fail. I mess up. I say something I shouldn't or do something I shouldn't. I get angry over spilled milk or I hold onto a harsh word spoken to me, instead of letting it go. I need practice each day but more than that, I need Jesus guiding me each day, changing me day by day. This happens little by little, even though most of the time I desire to change in leaps and bounds.

Sometimes I think God allows us to go through the wilderness seasons because He's trying to teach us something or because something we go through is going to help someone else. In those wilderness times, pray and ask God what He wants to show you. Ask Him what you can learn from the experience or what He's going to use it for. Don't let that time be wasted but instead see what God is doing in and through you. Through my own struggles God has shown me things that I can use to help those around me, sometimes my kids or my friends. I want to share some of these lessons with you to help you as you go through your struggle.

1. Get rid of a defeatist mindset

If I determine in my mind that I'm going to persevere no matter what, I enjoy the journey more than if I allow feelings or thoughts of defeat to come in (following my feelings). I am not saying I enjoy the journey of struggle while I'm in it *but* I have an easier time navigating through when I keep my mind determined towards conquering rather than saying things like, "I don't know if I can get through this," or "if God doesn't take this away today, I won't be able to trust Him." Those types of statements are not only poisonous to your relationship with God but they also poison your mind, your determination and your journey becomes even harder because you're allowing your thoughts to dictate your feelings and ultimately your actions. I have instead learned that no matter what I'm facing, when I put my *trust and hope* in Jesus, I know that although the journey may be trying and painful at times, God will give me the strength I need to endure it. It changes my mindset and it allows me to walk in a greater level of peace and hope than if I have a defeatist mindset.

2. Stop allowing your feelings to dictate your day

You don't have to follow your feelings. Say, for example, I don't 'feel' like cleaning the dishes, I have that option. I can choose to do it later. But if the next day, and the next day, and the next three weeks, I continue to not do the dishes, not only will I have no dishes left to use, I will have an enormous mess instead of a few quick dishes had I taken care of it the first day. If I leave it for those three weeks because I don't feel like it, I will pay more greatly for it in the future. I might not feel like doing it the first day but if I keep following my feelings, not only will I be dreading those dishes every day for those three weeks, I will have lost out on the joy of accomplishing that task. Rather than 'feeling' like doing the dishes, I make my mind up to do them and I complete the task, following through on my decision. Similarly, if I make the choice to trust God's Word and His promises instead of my feelings, I am going to reap a greater reward. Rather than following my feelings that twist and turn all over the place, leading me down multiple rabbit holes, I make up my mind that I'm going to trust God, trust what He says in His Word and keep my eyes focused on Him. I may not enjoy the struggle, I may still find it hard, but I have small victories in knowing I'm not alone and that God is at work, fighting my battles (2 Chronicles 20:15) and taking care of me.

Launching You Into Your Next Victory

I know the path may be rough right now. There are boulders to climb. It may feel like the blaze of the summer sun is unrelentingly scorching your back; your skin dry and tight. Your lips are parched and dry, cracking and crying out for water. Your feet are weary from the trek as step by step you lug yourself along, unsure of your strength to endure. That is how it can feel while you're in the middle of it all. You may be in the middle of the journey, or at the beginning or the end. It doesn't matter where you're at in your journey of pain, or struggle. What matters is who you keep your eyes on while you're in the middle of it all. When your eyes are focused on Jesus bringing you through, rather than focusing on the problem, your faith and hope are restored and the problem begins to shrink. I have seen this so many times in my own struggles; it's amazing what happens when Christ displaces worry at the centre of your life, just like it's put so beautifully in Philippians 4:6-7 in *The Message* version, "Don't fret or worry. Instead of worrying, pray. Let petitions and praises shape your worries into prayers, letting God know your concerns. Before you know it, a sense of God's wholeness, everything coming together for good, will come and settle you down. It's wonderful what happens when Christ displaces worry at the centre of your life."

> When your eyes are focused on Jesus bringing you through, rather than focusing on the problem, your faith and hope are restored and the problem begins to shrink.

It may seem premature to say it now, but I do think it needs to be said: we cannot always understand why these trials happen. We often don't get to see the big picture like God does, we may not ever know the 'why,' and the sooner you can come to grips with that truth, the sooner you will begin to let go of control and instead give it to God.

Freedom will be available when you understand God has purpose in it all. You can allow Him to freely steer the ship without you telling Him where He should go.

CHAPTER 10

Don't Stuff Those Feelings

Something that needs to be said on the topic of suffering, struggle and trials is that even though a lot of this book talks about what you need to do—to help change your mindset and to be strong, victorious and courageous—there is another side that's very important, too. Yes, part of getting through the struggle is being determined, making your mind up that you will be strong and you will persevere with the help of Jesus.

But you also should not ignore another side, a preemptive step to this process. And that is *being real with yourself about your feelings;* not stuffing your feelings inside and ignoring the process. Sometimes it's a process of grieving or other times it's a matter of processing the situation. If you ignore this first step, all the other steps proceeding it will be useless.

It's not a whole lot different than the cylce involved in the grieving process of the death of a loved one. Although the situation may be different, the steps are very similar. You cannot simply skip steps and fast-forward to the end, hoping that you'll be able to avoid the process and feelings in-between. You have to go through the awkward and uncomfortable feelings in order to come out whole on the other side.

Think of it like patching a boat. If there is a hole in the boat, the captain cannot simply cover the hole with whatever material he feels like. He cannot use a wad of gum to patch a hole. It may hold temporarily but eventually water will get in. Instead, he has to go through the process of preparing the hole, using the correct materials, taking the necessary time to dry between layers, sanding and repeating the process until the last and final step. If he skips any of the steps, it will eventually catch up with him and the boat will spring a leak due to an improper patch job.

Similarly, if we try to skip the steps of being honest with our feelings or the process, we miss out on a full recovery. We have to take the time to begin by addressing how we feel, being honest with ourselves about the anger or frustration, resentment or worry, bitterness or sadness. We should not simply say, 'It's fine, I'll get over it.' Doing so would be like putting a wad of gum in the boat's hole. We must take the time to process our feelings as a first step.

Processing your feelings can look different to different people. For some it may be spending some time hiking, praying to God, or journaling their thoughts/prayers, or spending time doing something creative. Still, for others it might be finding a trusted friend, or a family member to pour your heart out to. And others may need to seek out counselling, preferably with a Christian counsellor or pastor. However you do it, you *need to take the time to do it*. Honour yourself enough to take the time.

There is no rush or magic number of days or weeks in which you need to accomplish this. Some may need a day, some may need a few days and others may need a few weeks or longer. If it's an issue that you haven't dealt with from the past, it won't just go away on its own. If it's something you never fully healed from you will need to readdress it in the present. The sooner you accept the situation and your feelings, the sooner you can begin to move through the rest of the process. But only you will know when it's time to move on.

When You Want to Give Up

There will be times when you feel like you want to give up. I know, because I've been there. It can feel like the weight of the problem is too much to handle. It may feel like no matter what positive or encouraging thing anyone says, or you read, it is not enough to convince you to believe the positive. There are moments when even the bravest of souls have their breaking point and begin to let the worry and fear creep in and they feel they just can't do it. I have been there. I have had those moments at the height of the pain.

I remember one incident in particular. It was in the middle of the health struggle I spoke of earlier and I had been hoping and praying for a positive change. I had been going through this up and down struggle for seven years. It can be hard to hold onto hope when you've been praying for years for a breakthrough. I had been trying to keep my hopes up that things would change, that I would finally be on the right path. The next time I had an appointment, I was told that although I had been on the upswing and doing better for a couple of weeks, I was now doing worse again. It was a gut punch, because I had actually begun to hope for good news, only to have them dashed. I was angry with myself for getting my hopes up. I can't explain why sometimes we feel the way we do, but we just need to understand that it's okay to be honest with what you're feeling.

I was so upset. I felt an entire range of emotions: let down, angry, worried, sad, frustrated…they kept cycling through in waves.

The next day we were going to go on a family drive to a nearby city and I just wasn't feeling up to it. I had let myself get down in the dumps and I didn't even have the energy to pick myself back up again. This wasn't typical for me as I'm usually very positive, upbeat and strong—the helper. But even the strong ones need a hand sometimes.

I had prayed about the situation from the previous day but at that point, I was just too tired to put effort towards anything: hope, prayer, expectation. I knew the trip with my family would tire me out and I chose to stay home. The moment everyone left, it all came out. The tears. The frustration. The anger. The deep, deep sorrow. I had been trying so hard to keep it all in that when I finally had a chance to let it go, boy did I let it fly. I sobbed so hard my eyes puffed up like a soggy biscuit. I went through what felt like 15 different emotions in a matter of an hour. But I needed to let it all out and I let it all out to God. I wasn't thinking about the perfect way to pray or what I should say; there was no eloquence, I just poured my heart out. It was freeing and exhausting, all at the same time. And God listened. He didn't argue with me or tell me to think about all the blessings I had, He just listened.

But at the same time I was crying, I desperately wanted to be with my family. I felt guilty for letting them down, and staying home. I was so, *so* angry that because of this health issue, it made me tired and not myself. It made me *so* tired each day. I was so deeply sorrowful that this precious time with my family was being robbed from me. The more I thought about that, the more upset I got. Even while I was crying, I thought to myself, *"Well I know it's not as bad as some people have it. It could be so much worse."* And, yes, it could be, but when you're in the midst of pain, someone else having worse pain doesn't negate your own. I didn't know what to think or feel; I was numb inside yet so aware of every thought, feeling and emotion.

I began to wonder if this was ever going to get any easier— if I was ever going to have the victory…if I could really…truly… keep my hopes up.

I would love to say to you that suddenly a miraculous experience ensued and changed my whole day! But there wasn't anything immediate like that. Sometimes God works that way but I would say more often than not, He lets us learn. How can we learn, if everything is done for us?

No, this story is not that kind of story. It's not a shiny red bow that I can neatly tuck into place. It's a practical, simple burlap ribbon, haphazardly lumped into a pile *resembling* a bow. I felt God clearly say to me, "This isn't all you're making it to be." And that may seem like an odd thing for God to say. You may think it sounds unusual to hear from a caring Father but the truth is that in that moment I was *lost* in my emotions and I needed Him to step in and speak some truth to me. I was beginning to think everything else was crashing down, too. I was not thinking rationally. Isn't that the way we can be sometimes? So caught up in our own emotions and feelings that we become overwhelmed and lose sight of the truth? I actually really needed to hear that, and He needed to step in and speak truth to me because we can make our molehills into mountains if we only follow our emotions. We need to be real with our feelings and emotions; we also need someone who can speak truth into the situation and speak some sense into our nonsensical world.

It caused me to stop; pause. I realized I had to make a choice. I realized that God couldn't make this decision for me, I needed to. He gave us free will and we can use it to choose good or evil. He can lead us to the water but ultimately we have to choose to drink it. I needed to express my feelings because I needed to be real with myself but there also comes an end to that time and we need to then move onto the next step. I had to ask myself: will I let my emotions and feelings rule me this way, or will I pick up the broken pieces and keep going on my way? Or better yet, because He is our Restorer, will I let God pick up my broken pieces and put them back together?

The truth is that we make the decision, but God is the only one who can put us back together. Somehow, He takes all the broken shards and tattered fragments and He gently pieces them all back together. But instead of Him making it look the way it was before it was broken, He carefully designs a beautiful mosaic that now emanates a different beauty. One that others can see and relate to. One that others look at with marvellous awe. One that looks nothing like the others and tells a story of resiliency, redemption and a God who lovingly fixes broken things.

So often our beautiful testimonies come out of the mucky mess. They come out of the hardships and the trials, the moments where it all comes to a head. The moments like I just described, above. Those are hard, hard moments but the beauty of it all is that they're *moments*. They pass. Eventually everything will pass. The pain. The struggle. The storm. The hardship. They may last longer than you planned or much longer than you'd like but just like it says in Ecclesiastes 3:1, for everything there is a season, and a time for every purpose under the sun.

I don't know what your struggle is right now. My prayer is that these words touch your heart and that God would use them to encourage you touch your heart if your heart is hurting right now. Nothing anyone can do or say will help or penetrate your heart unless you make the decision to keep going, unless you decide that you're going to let someone 'speak sense into your nonsensical world." Because the truth is, things don't make sense when you're struggling. Trials don't make sense. Feelings don't make sense. The *'why'* question begs you for an answer, constantly knocking at your door and pulling on your shirt like a toddler whining to be picked up. You don't often understand why and you want answers. But answers won't change your circumstances. And answers won't make your circumstances feel better. Instead, you have to make a decision to trust that God is there to help you put the pieces back together. Make that decision right now. And pray. Pray your little heart out to God with all that you're feeling and struggling with. He *will* speak to you and He *will* guide and direct you. It *will* be just the thing you need to hear. Even if it's not what you expected Him to say, it's what your heart is longing to hear.

As I've mentioned before, I have had many struggles in my life, some intense and some that quietly putter in the background. It used to take me weeks to really accept some situations but I can say that with the help of God, I have been able to accept the hard circumstances with a quicker approach than I used to. It used to really set me back, emotionally, and I would play the emotions and feelings through my head; however, as God has built up my 'struggle muscles' and made me more resilient, and as I have leaned on *God* to be my strength rather than myself, it takes less time for me to accept my circumstances so that I can then move on and begin tackling the other steps.

What are these others steps I am speaking of? The steps are:
- Trusting in God in the Midst of the Storm
- Letting Go of Reasoning and Bitterness
- Digging into the Word and Believing What it Says For You and Your Life
- Prayer and Petition
- A Grateful Attitude

I will go into more detail about each step and how these steps will help you walk through the process of struggle.

Trusting God in the Midst of the Storm

First and foremost, you cannot keep relying on yourself. You have to surrender your circumstances and your will to God. You need to just make that decision and ***do*** it. No more waffling. Either you trust God or you don't. But choosing to trust Him to take care of you and lead you down the path and out of the wilderness isn't a feeling, it's a ***choice***. I can't stress that enough. It's a ***choice***. And it's the best one you can make.

Letting Go of Reasoning and Bitterness

As we talked about in Chapter 3 and 4, these two things (bitterness and resentment) will stop you from progressing at all. The key is: the middle of the struggle is not the time to stop. It's not the time to plop yourself down on a boulder and stop journeying along. If you *do*, that's exactly the place where you will find yourself years from now: ***stuck***. Like, deep-in-the-mud-need-a-tow-truck kind of stuck. It's the place where the enemy likes to come in and tell you you can't do it, it's never going to get better and that you should be angry with God for letting this happen. The enemy will convince you that you should feel bad for yourself and find someone to blame. You will find that instead of momentarily stopping there for a break, you will have a pity party for yourself and you may end up camping there or even worse, taking up permanent residence.

The truth is that we all understandably want to avoid suffering in any way possible, but human nature will quickly step in and you may begin to feel bad for yourself and have feelings of pity for yourself, perhaps even feeling justified in your attitude. The enemy will take that and whisper lie upon lie on top of it, and before long you've believed a lot of lies and are losing sight of the truth. I know of what I speak, because that's what led me to losing sight of God's love for me when I've been in the middle of some of my struggles. I stayed put there too long, not even realizing I was, and the enemy used that to twist the truth. Roots of bitterness, resentment and anger grew.

But just like it says in Romans 8:28, God can work out good from our bad situations, and you know how He does that? He uses them as teachable moments for me. He shows me exactly where I've stumbled and then He shows me the way out. I am able to use that as a teaching tool not only for myself, but to help encourage you and show you the roadmap of not only what to do but what *not* to do. God took my hardship and He turned it into something good that will be used for His glory! Isn't that an amazing promise that we have as believers? God can take a bad situation, and work good out of it!

Joyce Meyer frequently emphasizes, "You don't have to park at the point of your pain," (qtd. by Daystar) and I would have to agree. Keep moving forward. Keep determining to move forward in your heart. And keep your eyes focused on Jesus, the author and perfector of our faith!! (Hebrews 12:2).

Digging into the Word and Believing What it Says For You and Your Life

The Word of God is *living* and *breathing* and more powerful than a double-edged sword. We don't have a lot of perspective of what that means because we don't live in a time period where swords are commonly used, but it's still a beautiful description of how the Word is used in our lives.

Rick Renner, an international evangelist, does an excellent job of explaining this in a practical way:

> "The phrase 'two-edged' is taken from the Greek word distomos and is unquestionably one of the oddest words in the entire New Testament. Why is it so odd? Because it is a compound of the word di, meaning two, and the word stomos, which is the Greek word for one's mouth. Thus, when these two words are compounded into one (distomos), they describe something that is two-mouthed! Don't you agree that this seems a little strange? So why would the Bible refer to the Word of God repeatedly as a 'two-edged sword' or, literally, a 'two-mouthed sword'? [...]
>
>   The Word of God is like a sword that has two edges, cutting both ways and doing terrible damage to an aggressor. Ephesians 6:17 calls it 'the sword of the Spirit, which is the word of God.' Here is an example: You are praying about a situation, and suddenly a Bible verse rises up from inside your heart. At that moment, you are consciously aware that God has given you a verse to stand on and to claim for your situation. You've received a word that came right out

of the mouth of God and dropped into your spirit! That word from God was so sharp that it cut right through your questions, intellect, and natural logic and lodged deep within your heart. [...]

After you meditated on that quickened word from God, it suddenly began to release its power inside you. Soon you couldn't contain it any longer! Everything within you wanted to declare what God had said to you. You wanted to say it. You want to release it out of your mouth! And when you did, those powerful words were sent forth like a mighty blade to drive back the forces of hell that had been marshalled against you, your family, your business, your ministry, your finances, your relationship, or your body.

First, that word came out of the mouth of God. Next, it came out of your mouth! When it came out of your mouth, it became a sharp, 'two-edged' — or literally, a 'two-mouthed' — sword. One edge of this sword came into existence when the Word initially proceeded out of God's mouth. The second edge of this sword was added when the Word of God proceeded out of YOUR mouth!

The Word of God remains a one-bladed sword when it comes out of God's mouth and drops into your heart but is never released from your own mouth by faith. That supernatural word simply lies dormant in your heart, never becoming the two-edged sword God designed it to be.

But something happens in the realm of the Spirit when you finally rise up and begin to speak forth that word. The moment it comes out of your mouth, a second edge is added to the blade! Nothing is more powerful than a word that comes first from God's mouth and then from your mouth. You and God have come into agreement, and that agreement releases His mighty power into the situation at hand" (Renner).

What this means is that we can have faith in the Word, and its use in our lives. It's no accident when you come across a Scripture that jumps out on the page to you. That's the Holy Spirit using the Word to speak directly into your life. That's what is meant when it says that the Word is alive.

In the context of struggle, God will give you confirmations and words that you can count on from the Bible. What I *love* about the Bible is that it's no one's opinion. It is truth. It is directly from the mouth of God and because of that fact, I can trust what it says and I can have confidence in what it's telling me. That is a beautifully important thing to be able to cling onto when you're in the midst of a struggle. It's just truth. From God's mouth to your heart. What greater comfort is there than that? 23:06 Ch 10

You have to believe the Word instead of your feelings. You must not simply read the Word and then when you feel discouraged, ignore the truth of what you read. You must make the decision to not follow your feelings, but to believe God's Word and that He is speaking to you through it.

Prayer and Petition

"Don't worry about anything; instead, pray about everything. Tell God what you need, and thank Him for all He has done. Then you will experience God's peace, which exceeds anything we can understand. His peace will guard your hearts and minds as you live in Christ Jesus" Philippians 4:6 (NLT).

This verse has always been an encouragement to me that no matter what I face, I don't have to face it afraid but I can instead face it with faith! This verse should be tattooed on our hearts so we never forget that God is with us.

God tells us that we do not need to be afraid in the storm, but instead we can always pray and ask Him for what we need.

We must not forget one of the most important parts about this verse and about your relationship with God, and that is this: it says, 'with thanksgiving' and it's there for a reason. We will talk about gratitude in our next step.

A Grateful Attitude

Think about it. Think about what gratitude does for your mindset and your outlook on life. Gratitude also keeps things in perspective and also praises God for what He's already done and what He will do.

There *are* things you can be thankful for when you're in the middle of the storm. I promise you there are. Think back to story of Corrie Ten Boom. Her sister told her to be thankful for the fleas. Corrie could not imagine being thankful for fleas (and I'm with you, Corrie!) but God works in mysterious ways and He used those fleas to protect the young women and allow them to share the gospel with their entire barrack. How many souls were saved because of some fleas? That is a perfect example to me of how we can be thankful and grateful, no matter what our circumstances. We not only need to recognize our gratefulness but also speak that to God and share our gratitude with Him. It's an incense of praise to Him and it changes our hearts and our mindsets in the process.

When you're tempted to believe that this is not going to get better, that it will never end or that God has left you alone in the situation, ask yourself if any of those things are true. Ask yourself if you can back that up with Scripture. Can you find those beliefs or promises anywhere in the Word? No, but you *can* find the opposite of those lies—the truth—in the Word. Everything has a season. Eventually everything comes to an end. Like it says in Ecclesiastes 3:1, "For everything there is a season, a time for every activity under heaven" (NLT). God is always with us and He is fighting our battles for us (2 Chronicles 20:15). We can stand on those truths rather than the thoughts and resulting feelings that the enemy tries to plant in our minds. Be strong in mind and heart, resisting the lies of the enemy. Stay alert: "Be sober-minded; be watchful. Your adversary the devil prowls around like a roaring lion, seeking someone to devour" (1 Peter 5:8, ESV) . Recognize that when you're in the middle of the storm, that is the most important time to stand on the truth of God's word. That's the pivotal point in which to draw close to Jesus. It says in James 4:8, that when we draw near to God, He will draw near to us. That has absolutely been my experience! He is nearer to us when we call out to Him; He is nearest to us when we are in the middle of the storm. He draws us close to Him while He comforts us. Be honest with your grief, your burden, your worry but then *give* it to Him. Let Him take it. His arms are equipped to carry our load and He wants us to give it to Him. Nowhere in Scripture does it tell us to carry our own burden. Give it to Him and don't take it back.

Step by step you'll be guided through this valley. Sometimes it may feel like a crawl but *at least* you're still moving forward. You're not parking at the point of your pain and stopping. You're not camping out on Pity Party Lane and you're at least moving forward, even if it's a slow crawl. Dig into the Word. Find promises and truth from the Word that you can meditate on and post around your house or on your phone. Write it on the tablet of your heart (Proverbs 7:3) so that you believe it *more* than you believe your feelings.

CHAPTER 11

Trusting, Still

One of the hardest parts of the journey is trusting in God, trusting His plan, and trusting while it still hurts—while you're still in the midst—while you're still standing in the middle of the storm, feet soaked and chilled to the bone, waiting for rescue. Those are the times when I believe your faith counts for double. Those are the moments when you have to give it all you've got: to hold onto faith and to hold onto Jesus.

There's something I've learned from walking through some tough storms. One of the most important lessons is that when I take my eyes off of Jesus the storm feels like it may overtake me. When I take my eyes off Jesus, that's when I begin to sink into the water. When I take my eyes off Him, that's when I begin to falter, stumble and lose hope.

But when I keep my eyes on Jesus…

I realize that He will give me the strength to endure, because I can do all things through Christ who *gives me strength*. He gives me the courage to decide that I'm going to persevere; I am able to take each step He gives me. When my eyes are on Jesus, I feel His love for me, surrounding me and hedging me in. I can feel Him go to battle for me, defeating my enemies and holding me close while I wait for Him to rescue me.

I have to keep my faith strong while I'm in the middle of the storm. But how do you do that when you're already feeling weak and vulnerable? We cannot unrealistically tuck struggle in a neat little box. But is it possible to be stronger in faith when you're in the midst of the storm more so than after you've received the victory?

The answer depends on you. It will take some effort on your part to *choose* to stand strong when inside, you feel like a limp spaghetti noodle, weak in the knees. You will need to *choose* to believe the Word of God, the promises of God, and that the Word is active in your life, even when it feels like your heart is paper-thin and you're holding on by a thread. I wish I could say something beautiful and eloquent that would make you comfortably slouch into the back of your chair like a child, curled up in a cozy fleece blanket, melting into the thick embrace of the chair. I would love to tell you anything to ease the discomfort, but I am not Jesus. Jesus is the only answer to these problems. He comes in and rescues us like no other. And we can rely and trust in Him to guide us out of the wilderness. Your part in that, though, is to trust Him and to keep your hope up, believing that Jesus is going to help you and you will come through victorious in the end.

The enemy will try to convince you of anything other than this. He doesn't want you to trust in Jesus; He wants you to doubt Him. The enemy may use a tainted word from someone or try to twist the truth but the one thing you can always rely, count on and trust in, is the Word of God; the sword of truth. When the enemy tries to tempt you to stop believing in hope or that you're never going to get out of this storm, keep standing on faith. Read these verses as a biblical confirmation of these truths:

> "No temptation has overtaken you except what is common to mankind. And God is faithful; He will not let you be tempted beyond what you can bear. But when you are tempted, He will also provide a way out so that you can endure it" 1 Corinthians 10:13 (NIV).

> "Therefore put on God's complete armor, that you may be able to resist and stand your ground on the evil day [of danger], and, having done all [the crisis demands], to stand [firmly in your place]" Ephesians 6:13 (AMPC).

Trust in Jesus is something I struggled with for many years after the long battle that I had. It was painful and while in the midst of it, I didn't rely on Jesus as much as I should or could have. I spent a lot of time trying to find my own way out. I did trust Jesus in many aspects, but not 100%. I always (even subconsciously) had a backup plan in my pocket, just in case. I *wanted* to trust in Him 100% but I was worried and afraid much of the time. My fear caused me to take my eyes off Jesus and His truth and promises, and look at the situation with human eyes and in doing so, I began to apply human reasoning to the situation. I would think things like, "I know God can do this but just in case, I will prepare myself for 'Plan B.'" I was placing my human understanding ahead of my faith.

When You're Tired of Waiting

Oh boy, have I been there. I can empathize, sympathize and "anything-else"-ize with you, here. The 'waiting room' and I were not even on speaking terms at one point because I really resented the waiting and not 'seeing the needle move' on my situation, so to speak. Sometimes the breakthroughs come quickly and other times they take a long time. The struggle I went through below, involved waiting two long years for a resolution. Of course, there were periods and seasons of victory within that timeframe, but it seemed like it was taking forever. That's when hope tends to pack its bags and hit the road.

I remember one of the seasons in that waiting room. I was doing all the things I was supposed to be doing, eating right, exercising, taking all the right supplements and minerals and vitamins and I was gaining weight at a steady rate. I have always lead a healthy lifestyle so it was very out of the ordinary for me. I went to my doctor, my naturopath, I prayed and believed in faith. I did anything and everything they recommended but the scale kept going up and up. Tests didn't reveal much but it was during the season when I was going through the big health struggle I spoke about earlier. Talk about adding yet another frustrating layer in the middle of an already very difficult season for me. I was patient and understanding at the beginning. But as time progressed and nothing I did stopped the weight from piling on, my patience began to run out. No one had answers for me. Nothing was helping, in fact it was getting worse and worse. Completely out of my control. Now you may be thinking this was a vanity issue but it was't so much that as it was a physical issue. Do you know what it's like to suddenly put on a few pounds a week, for many months? When they keep adding up and you cannot stop it? What it feels like to look in your closet and realize almost all your clothes are unwearable because they no longer fit? What it feels like to go for a walk when you're essentially carrying a few sacks of potatoes around your waist? It's hard on you emotionally, yes, but it's even harder on you physically. And nothing I did stopped it.

This went on for almost two years. I was holding out faith that it would just miraculously disappear. That I would just start seeing some movement but I didn't. I definitely had faith in God that He would bring me the answers I needed but I also began to get impatient at the year and a half mark. I was feeling terribly physically and at times, emotionally. I knew in my spirit and in my heart that God was in control and at work. I trusted His plan. I knew it was going to be His timing not mine, but I still had moments of frustration.

There was one day in particular when I went for a walk and my clothes felt so tight on my body that I burst out in tears and felt like my heart was a balloon that had just been deflated. I felt like I was a stranger in my own body. I felt so helpless in the situation. Helpless to stop, helpless to know what was going on. Just so helpless.

Have you had those feelings visit you during your pain and struggle? Are you feeling them right now? Feelings of helplessness and lack of control can lead down a spiralling staircase of anxiety and worry if we don't pay attention or recognize our feelings. It's so hard, not knowing *if* it's going to end. How many times have you wished for a glimpse into the future? I would pray things like, "God, if I could just know that it's all going to work out in the end, then I can wait but not knowing if it's ever going to end feels like more than I can bear." When you're in that place of waiting you just want assurance. You want help. You want to be rescued.

How does one wait 'well'? How does one wait while walking into the unknown? How does one step forward in courage and leave worry behind? How does one journey forward without knowing the outcome? Will you be the victor or the spoil? How do you praise God while lying there in pain? How do you thank God when you're really angry at your circumstances? How?

I know you're expecting me to give you a well-laid out plan now. That sure would be nice. I don't have all the perfect answers you seek. I'm sorry. Because your answers will be different than mine. But when I was in that place, I took each of these questions to God. I didn't know what to do and I sure didn't know how to 'wait well.' I didn't know my right foot from my left at times and I really needed direction on how to proceed with faith and trust.

One thing that God reminded me of was Matthew 6:8b: "Your Father knows what you need before you ask him." That really spoke to my heart. I can pray and agree with God's will but ultimately He is at work and He knows what I need. He's a good Father who gives His children good gifts, and He knows what we need. That was a real comfort to my heart. I kept this verse nearby and it was a beautiful reminder for me.

Secondly, God reminded me that I didn't need to keep 'doing' things in order to receive an answer or healing. I think we get caught up in trying to work our own way out of the pit that we forget to let God do the work. We keep trying to do things on our own. God didn't need me to direct traffic for Him. He needed me to trust and wait. If He showed me something to do then I could do it but more often than not, He asks us to wait and trust in Him. Even if it takes time for your feelings to catch up, make that decision to surrender. God wants to work your problem out but He's going to do is His way (which is the best way anyways) and me trying to rush Him won't cause Him to rush. I needed to decide to get out of God's way, surrender and make a decision to let Him do it His way, in His timing. When I was trying to figure out the problem, I spent time searching for answers and worrying, rather than turning those worries into prayers.

Third, I had to come to the realization that as much as I wanted my circumstances to change, God doesn't owe me. Nothing is owed to me. Any of the blessings that I have in my life are because of

God's goodness, grace and mercy, not because of anything I've done or earned. His gifts to me are just that: gifts. Gifts are not earned, they've given out of love. God reminded me that peace doesn't come from within self, it comes from above. All gifts come from above. "Every good and perfect gift is from above, coming down from the Father of the heavenly lights, who does not change like shifting shadows" (James 1:17 NIV). Resolve, joy, peace, goodness, favour, blessing—all those gifts don't come from within myself, they come from above, from God. I don't need to keep striving for things that God freely gives. I can rest in knowing He will give me what I need, when I need it. He will provide me with peace when my heart is troubled (John 14:27). He will provide me with joy when I am sad. He will provide me with the victory when I am feeling defeated. I don't need to micromanage or strive from within myself, I need to instead ask Him to give me what I need to get through this. And He did. Even though it went on longer than I would have liked, God did step in and reveal answers to the doctors and it was amazing to see God's hand at work as day by day I felt better, and better. I knew God had given me the breakthrough I desired and I was so thankful.

Lastly, God spoke something really profoundly to me. I'm going to use an illustration that He gave me and I think it really demonstrates this point well.

Have you ever been to an escape room? They are these fantasy rooms, set up like a bedroom or a scene and you're locked into this room with a group (4-5 people), given a time limit and told that in order to be let out of the room, you need to solve all the riddles. As you solve the first riddle, you get a clue for the next one. This goes on a number of times until you finally solve the last clue and you can then 'escape' the room and be let out. It's such a fun game and I've done it a few times with friends. At first you don't know what to expect but once you get into the rhythm of solving the riddles it becomes such a blast to see how quickly you can solve them and be released.

There are a few key things to note about escape rooms. They're timed. You only have a certain amount of time to solve the riddles and get out of the room or you fail the escape. Also, there are a number of rules you have to follow when in the room. There is also an immense amount of adrenaline and pressure you feel when you're in the midst of the game because you know you're running against the clock. But most importantly and lastly, to succeed, you have to earn your way out. It's not a given. You must earn it.

Sometimes being in the middle of a struggle can feel like being held in an escape room—the waiting room. You want to get out of the struggle. When you're working in your own strength you have to get all the answers right and you're working against a timer—the pressure is immense but you're sure if *you* work at it hard enough, you can earn your way to freedom. But God revealed something to me about struggle and hardship that has altered the way that I wait. *With God, we don't have to **earn** our way out of the struggle.* Freedom is a gift and one that He's more than willing to give. Instead, while we wait on Him, trust in Him and have faith that He is at work, He lines up all the circumstances and timing and we just get to walk out. No timer. No pressure. No list of 'good deeds' to excuse you. It's not earned. It's a gift. That changed my entire perspective on the aforementioned, previously dreaded 'waiting room.' After that point, the waiting room still wasn't as appealing to me as say, a bar of beautifully crafted chocolate, but as I waited on God to provide me with what I needed for my period of waiting—peace, endurance, trust—contentment began to fill my heart and I knew that I could wait yet another day.

The Faith Walk

Faith is mentioned so often that it almost loses its meaning, at least that was the case for me. Do we fully *understand* the gift of faith or how it works in our lives? I knew what faith was but I didn't realize that I wasn't exercising it very often. I would pray my prayer, asking God to work in a situation and then it's almost as if I would forget or ignore my prayer and then go ahead and do what *I* thought would solve the problem. I wasn't putting my faith in God at all, but rather I was putting my faith in myself or my abilities. That led to a lot of worry and stress, and ultimately a lot of heavy emotional pressure because we are in far less control than we think we are. We think that if we can control the situation, we will be confident and have a positive outcome but so much of what we think we are in control of, we are not.

Control is not as intoxicatingly delicious as we think it is. It leads to a cycle of anxiety when things don't go as planned and it can lead to alienation of those close to you.

Control is a strange beast. It's like the man who makes his first million. He tells himself that once he reaches that goal of one million dollars, he will be satisfied. But once he reaches that goal, one million isn't enough anymore. He wants more. He craves more. He has an appetite for more. It begins to consume him and once he has reached that insatiable appetite for more money, it causes stress and puts a strain on relationships and his own personal happiness.

Nothing is so alluring as that which we can't have. It's something in our human nature. But it doesn't have to control us. We can be aware of it and do the opposite and by daily surrendering control to God and surrendering control in all areas of our lives, we show God respect and honour, giving Him the authority to be in charge. Who would you rather have in charge? God—who is good, who knows and sees everything—or yourself, who can barely see past the end of your own nose?

The truth is that even if you don't *want* to give up control, you simply cannot control all your circumstances. That's the reality—even if you don't want to believe it's true. Sorry to burst that bubble. It's why I find it beautiful what Paul said in Philippians 4:11, "for I have learned to be content whatever the circumstances" *(NIV)*, because we need to learn to be content no matter what the circumstances are. But it takes effort. As Paul said it's a *learned behaviour*.

People often think the opposite of control is surrender, and I would absolutely agree with that but I would say that what also goes hand in hand with surrender, is trust…in God. In His plan, His timing and His ability to give us what we need. People who struggle with having control are often trying to overcompensate because they feel out of control in other areas. For example, someone who cannot lose weight may struggle with controlling food or go to extremes with food. But surrender is not limited to just one area. Full surrender is a relinquishing of control in all areas and in all ways.

It's easy to fall into that pattern of control but it doesn't mean you have to stay there. Learning to trust God to provide for all your needs and daily surrendering to Him will bring you such peace. As Jesus promises in John 14:27, "Peace I leave with you; My peace I give you. I do not give to you as the world gives. Do not let your hearts be troubled and do not be afraid" (NIV). It may take some time for peace to come, but once you take the pressure off of yourself to be in control of everything (which is really out of your control anyway) you will see the beauty and the privilege of trusting in God.

The other blessing in learning to surrender control to God is that you can be assured that no matter what the outcome is, God is still going to walk you through it. You aren't left to walk it alone. Your hand is forever being held by the Saviour, walking you through each step. You can trust in knowing that God is leading you step by step, even right now. In whatever you're going through. Right now that may not change your mind about how hard it is, but it will bring you some sense of peace to know you're not going through this alone.

No one wants bad news. No one wants heartache. It's excruciating and painful and no one would choose it. But somehow, if you can see Jesus in the storm with you, there's a glimmer of hope and a raindrop of peace. And that hope and peace is the lifeline that helps get you through the darkest days, in the middle of the heaviest storm.

I know it's asking a lot—to expect anyone who's going through heartache—to say that they can find hope and peace in the situation. It doesn't seem fair. It leads some to be angry with God, asking Him how He could ever allow such a thing. There are moments of rage and moments of deep-rooted sorrow and weeping. Be honest with God about those feelings. Tell Him, say it out loud. He already knows your feelings anyway. You can be real, raw and open with God. He wants you to call out to Him! But also in that, He wants you to have open arms to receive what He's going to do in your situation. It may not be what you have planned for yourself. It may not be the outcome you had expected. But I promise you that God only has **good** plans for you (Jeremiah 29:11) and if you know that, deep down on the inside of you, in your soul, then you can trust that even though you may not be able to see the way out, or you may not be able to understand any of why this happened or what is going on, God does. He knows. This day was not a surprise to Him, your situation was not a surprise to Him. He knows the way out; He's been preparing it. He listens. He catches all those tears. And He cares. He cares so deeply for you. He loves you, you're His child. Of that, you can have confidence and be assured.

Trusting in Him, while you're in the midst of the storm isn't going to feel easy. In fact, you will need to choose not to base decisions off of your feelings. Remember that your feelings are fickle, they change constantly and they are not reliable. Instead you need to make the decision to trust Him and hold fast to it. Don't waiver when you feel like you're not getting the desired result. Remember that He works all things for good, for those who love Him (Romans 8:28) and you can be assured that this struggle is not beyond His ability to work good!

It is often while you're waiting and trusting in God, hoping for the right result, that the enemy loves to come in and plant doubt in your mind. The *waiting room* I call it. That's when he hopes to catch you off guard. The enemy wants you to believe that it won't get any better, that you should meddle in the situation…that you know best. Well…it wasn't true when he told it to Eve and it isn't true now, either. You need to hold onto what God has told you and have hope in the promises in His word. Let that be your d*eciding guide*—knowing you can stand firm and hold onto the truth. If you know the truth then you don't have to believe the lies. One cancels out the other.

When I was in high school, I loved chemistry. I wasn't even good at math and science in general but chemistry was my jam! I loved it. Do you know why? Because I *loved* balancing equations. In chemistry, to make a chemical reaction work, it needs to be balanced on both sides of the equation. It wouldn't work if one of the sides was unbalanced. Also, what you add to one side of the equation, you must subtract from the other side or the equation won't be successful. I loved that idea of balance equalling success.

Similarly, we are more peaceful in our walk with God when we keep the balance in check. We cannot become extreme on one side and be swayed by opinions and ideals. We need to balance that out by being rational and listening to what God says. If you hold true to the truth then the lies will disappear. You add in the truth of God's Word and His promises for you, and what you hear Him saying to you and in doing so, you subtract the lies. You cannot believe a lie if you know the truth. The truth cancels out the lie.

If you know the truth then you don't have to believe the lies.

It says in Hebrews 12:1-2, "Therefore, since we are surrounded by such a great cloud of witnesses, let us throw off everything that hinders and the sin that so easily entangles. And let us run with perseverance the race marked out for us, fixing our eyes on Jesus, the pioneer and perfecter of faith." This verse reminds us that it's not always going to be easy. The example of running a race brings to mind thoughts of exhaustion and tired muscles and running out of breath, but it also evokes feelings of exhilaration and a sense of accomplishment and joy in finishing the race. There will be times in our walk when it's a struggle, when it seems too hard to keep going, just like any marathon runner knows. But there are also the times when we conquer and we win—a deep sense of accomplishment settles on us and God is right there with us, sharing in our joy. He was right there cheering you on the whole way through the race, giving you the ability to do it. God will always give you grace for what you're going through. He will make a way for you because that's the promise of our loving Father (2 Corinthians 12:9).

Open and closed doors

One of the ways God leads us is by either opening or closing doors. I'm sure you've heard the saying, "When God closes a door, somewhere He opens a window." I think this is quaint and charming and full of lovely sentiment. And the point it's trying to make is that even when we come up against a closed door, God will open up another way. I am being picky with the phrasing here but I would say this statement would be more accurate: "When God closes a door, don't try to push it open. Accept that, and know He will open a different door, a much better door." Clearly mine is not as poetic as the first, but I think we must be careful not to assume that a closed door is a bad thing. A door that has been closed by God—believe me—you don't want to open it. God is protecting you from something. Something that is perhaps bad for you, or worse than it could be. Or perhaps it's because He's got something even better in store for you, that you aren't even aware of yet. We aren't supposed to analyze the doors and presume to know why. That's where the 'trusting, still' comes in. Remind yourself: "Even though I thought this was what God wanted me to do, He's closed that door and I trust His plan." "Even though I thought I was supposed to take that route, clearly God's got a better one for me." We need to change the narrative in our mind from our narrow-minded thinking to instead trusting in knowing that God sees it *all*. He can see the beginning from the end and all the itty-bitty details in-between. If we knew it all, we wouldn't need God and so in trusting in Him, we give Him the glory for what He does. We can be thankful before we even see the victory because we know that He's in control and He has worked out the best possible plan for us.

Trusting while waiting for the victory isn't an easy walk. It's riddled with doubt at times and it's wrought with frustration, if I'm being blunt about it. I won't tell you that you will find it easy. Or perhaps you will! And that would be wonderful. But the truth is that it's hard to keep trusting when you're in the midst of it. Hope seems like a long-lost relative and the enemy tries to attack our minds by planting thoughts of negativity and doubt. One thing that I believe is so key that I've spoken about in my first book, *Fearless Victor*, is our thoughts are powerful and important. If we have a polluted mind with lots of negative thoughts, we will have a polluted outlook on life. If we keep our thoughts pure and lovely like it says in Philippians 4:8, then we are going to have more hope and expectancy. The cool thing about living in this time is that these biblical principles are now being backed by medical evidence, proving their efficacy. God has been trying to teach us for generations the principles of casting our cares, rest and cultivating pure thoughts. Now with the advances of science, neuroscientists have been able to prove just how scientifically accurate and fruitful that is. I think it's pretty neat to live in a time when we get to see this!

Neuroplasticity essentially describes the ability of your mind to adapt and change based on your thoughts, choices and feelings and is being widely discussed. There is a whole field of study dedicated to this now and the literature out there is amazing. Dr. Caroline Leaf is one of the leading influences in this space. She's a Christian neuroscientist who's dedicated her life to learning about the brain and the mind, pertaining to their connection. Her research indicates that the brain and the mind are in fact separate and that our mind actually controls our brain. For so many years, people have believed their thoughts were a result of their physical chemistry but through study and research they have found that's just not the case. If you can control your mind, you can control how your brain reacts. It's quite fascinating stuff and although I won't be going into depth about this particular subject in this book, I wanted to bring it to your attention because I think it's a really powerful tool that we have access to. I would encourage you to listen to her podcasts, or perhaps read her book, *Switch On Your Brain.* She loves to share the Word of God in her book and connect that to the science she has researched. When you are going through a hard time, finding resources is so important to help support you in your journey. Pray about it and see if this is something that God wants you to learn more about. Trust that He's led you to this time, place and even this page and seek His direction on which doors He's opening and closing on your path to victory.

The reason I bring up your thought life is because you cannot truly have victory if you are feeling trapped in your own mind. When you're going through a hard time, you're more susceptible to negative thinking, worry, fear and sadness. This is when the Bible says to guard your hearts and minds in Christ Jesus (Philippians 4:7).

It's important to become more aware of our thinking and to really evaluate our thoughts. Evaluate the conclusions we come to, regularly, in the situations that occur in life. We are surrounded by a culture today that subscribes to the mentality, "get them before they get us." What I mean by that is there's so much hostility arising in our culture, or competitiveness. Thing like who's thinner than who, or who's the better competitive sport player. This constant competitive mindset out in the world is pitting people against each other and that translates into negatively changing our mindsets if we aren't careful. We see what goes on in the world and we begin to adopt these mentalities for ourselves, often subconsciously and without realizing it.

That's why it is so important to evaluate your thoughts and your mindsets often. You may be adopting mindsets and even lies of the enemy that you didn't realize you were because they just sort of snuck in there. But if you constantly evaluate your mind you're more likely to catch those negative thinking patterns or lies.

If we are having our minds renewed and submitted to the Lord, then we are asking God to show us where we've adopted lies either from the world or lies of the enemy. He *will* show you if you ask. He will reveal the truth to you. Ask Him now and be open to what you hear Him saying to your heart.

I remember one specific time when I was having this odd feeling of something being off. I couldn't put my finger on it over the course of two days and I hadn't really spent any time in prayer about it. I assumed it would just go away. But it didn't. And the more I thought about it, the more it was bothering me. I was so frustrated, though, because I couldn't figure out what it was. I realized I should pray about this and so I did. I remember I had just dropped off my kids at a friend's house for a playdate and as I drove home I began to ask God what was going on with me. I felt like I was aimlessly drifting and I didn't know why. I asked Him to show me what was bothering me and asked Him to speak to me.

I got home and I began to pray and journal as I often do, and as I was, God began revealing that I needed to be reminded of who I am in Him. See, two months prior, I quit my professional career as a teacher. That's another story for another day but needless to say, making a big, life-altering decision like that was not an easy one. I had wrestled with it for over a year but after much prayer and discussion with my husband, we both agreed we felt this was what God wanted me to do. And so I did.

Little did I know that two months later I would be confronted with the emotions of that big decision. I realized I had believed that some of my worth, purpose and identity was wrapped up in that job and so in resigning from that job, emotionally, I felt like a piece of my worth, purpose and identity was gone. Needless to say, I didn't realize that on a conscious level until God showed me. And as I was able to put emotions and words to what I had been feeling, the unsettled feeling began to leave me and God swept in and reminded me in whom my worth, purpose and identity was found: Him. I cannot tell you what a blessing it was to have peace and be able to pray about the situation and let God come into it, to remind me who I am and give me fresh eyes to see that His plans for me weren't done yet. Even though that chapter had closed, a whole new one was beginning.

It's so easy to attach our identity, worth or purpose to what we do, but as God so beautifully reminded me, none of those compare to who we are in Christ. What matters is who He says we are. What matters is that we submit our lives to God and in doing that, He directs our paths and our steps. What matters is that He loves us so deeply that we don't need to do a single thing in order for Him to keep loving us. We attach so much of our worth and value to things in this world but it's all empty! Our purpose is in what God asks us to do, the big things but absolutely the small things, too! Being a loving mother to your children or helping the neighbour next door: those things don't necessarily seem like 'kingdom work' but God uses situations just like that to be His hands and feet. Don't discount what you're doing in life. If your heart is surrendered to God's will, He *will* lead, guide and direct you (Proverbs 16:9).

I share that story because it was a reminder to me about how important it is to bring my mind, emotions and mindsets to God. For the big stuff and the small stuff. And even more than that, I realized that as I looked back over my 'thought life' the two months leading up to that day, I had allowed myself to believe that my job *was* a part of my identity, purpose and value. Not realizing that I had been allowing those thoughts to circulate through my mind, there was a point at which my mindset shifted and I began to believe it. I think we do this often. We allow ideals or thoughts, or even the enemy's lies (which we don't always recognize) to sit long enough in our mind that it begins to take root and become a mindset.

Much in the same way, I believe that is how we let wrong mindsets come into play when it comes to questioning God loving or caring for us. We know His character and we know His love yet once a wrong mindset starts to take root, it changes the DNA of our thoughts. Added to that, the enemy is the father of lies and he wants to confuse us and force wrong mindsets to take root in hopes that it will turn us away from God or cause us to be angry or question God. Thankfully, we have the Holy Spirit who comes in and speaks truth to us and in doing so, we can be restored to relationship with God, repenting of our wrong thoughts and our wrong mindsets.

Wrong thoughts are going to happen because we live in a fallen world that has a very skewed view in many areas. It's part of the reality of living in this fallen world but the more watchful we are, the more quickly we are able to let God speak the truth to us and change them. We need to be watchful and regularly assess our thought life. We constantly need to submit our minds to Christ and learn to think like He does, but there is always a part of the human side of us that doesn't want to surrender. It's the constant struggle between spirit and flesh. But what I am saying is that part of being watchful is to regularly assess your thoughts and evaluate if something doesn't feel right. If you're like me, and you can't put your finger on it, pray about it. Ask God to show you what's bothering you. I know He will! He is faithful…that's who He is! He is truth, He is love, He is generous with His children. He wants to talk with you and expose the truth so that you can begin to walk in peace and be set free from any wrong mindsets or lies of the enemy. Take each situation to Him in prayer. Don't let it fester or wait to talk when it's an opportune time. Take the time to bring it to Him in prayer the moment you notice it and let the Healer go to work in your heart, soul, mind and emotions.

We need to be aware of when we are weaker in any way (physically, or spiritually), we must purpose time to spend with God and let Him protect our heart and minds from the temptation of the enemy. The enemy is the father of lies and he will try to deceive you in any way possible. He doesn't want to see you victorious, he wants to see you fail and suffer. It is therefore crucial that when you're feeling weak, you need to stand firm in your faith and ask God to be your strength. He promises that He will in 2 Corinthians 12:9: "'My grace is all you need. My power works best in weakness.' So now I am glad to boast about my weaknesses, so that the power of Christ can work through me."

You have hope and you don't need to be afraid that when you're struggling you will be at the mercy of the devil. Instead, pray and ask God to be your strength, and He will give you the strength you need to resist the devil—and then the beautiful promise is that the enemy *will flee*! Be simple in your prayer—you can even just say, "God, help me!" There have been times when I've been so unsure of what to do or say or pray, that I have just said, "God, help. Help," and He does! Sometimes He sends a friend to encourage me or He sends a word through a friend. Sometimes He gives me the most perfect devotional for that day. Other times He will give me a verse that I know in my spirit is just what He wanted to say to me. But whatever it is, don't try to do it alone. Let God come in and fight your battles for you. You're not meant to do it alone. He doesn't say anywhere in Scripture that you should try on your own. Instead, He keeps saying to cast your cares, to give Him the burden, to let Him be your strength when you're weak.

Above all else He says that when we trust in Him, we can do all things *through* Him. What a beautiful blessing to know that this mountain that seems like Everest is not too hard for you. He will make a way for you and lead you on the path out.

As you wait and rest, and as you trust in God to take you up and over this mountain, keep praying. Keep reading and studying the Word. Keep your eyes open for the times God shows up with a word for you or an encouragement. Take notice and see the strength He is giving you. Isaiah 41:10, where God says "I will strengthen you and help you; I will uphold you with my righteous right hand," is not a flimsy attempt to just make you think you can do it. It is a supernatural gift in which God provides us with the strength we need, whether physically, mentally or emotionally. Wait on Him, rely on Him, ask Him for help and trust that He will be faithful to come to your rescue.

Just like it says in Romans 4:18, " [For Abraham, human reason for] hope being gone, hoped in faith." That's what we need to do. Hope on in faith. Oh Lord, help us to hope on in faith! And trust that our God, who loves us so deeply, will show up and fight our battles for us!

It says in Proverbs 13:12, "Hope deferred makes the heart sick, but a longing fulfilled is a tree of life" (NIV). I would argue to say that truer words have never been spoken. When you've been waiting on an answer to prayer or a breakthrough and it hasn't come yet, it can be easy to give up hope. And once hope has been lost in your heart, it is a terrible feeling. If you've been praying and asking God for an answer but it's been a long wait, I understand exactly what you're going through. You have likely experienced all the things I've talked about in this book and more, because I have felt those same feelings. Anger, disappointment, bitterness, impatience, frustration, hopelessness. I have parked myself at each of their doorsteps, a time or two. I have dug my heels in and wrestled, like Jacob, refusing to leave without God's blessing. I have made pleas and prayed eloquent prayers; I have fasted and I have thrown myself at the mercy of God, placing all my emotions and tears at His feet, waiting for Him to sweep in and deliver me.

And while God has heard and seen all of those prayers, I have learned something in the waiting. It doesn't rush God. It doesn't hurry His timing or His plan along. What happens instead is God draws nearer to me and He comforts me *while* I wait. I think we are often too preoccupied with God doing it our way and in our timing and so we forget to honour His Sovereignty. We forget that He knows what's best. We forget that He is *always* good. Not sometimes…but always.

I have learned in those times of waiting and trusting for the victory, that I don't need to have the victory in order to praise Him. I don't need to have the victory to be content. I don't need to have the victory to honour and thank Him for all the other blessings in my life. I have learned that in my all-consuming, preoccupation with wanting the circumstances to change—now—I missed out on seeing the blessings God had placed right under my nose. I lost my ability to be grateful in the small things, in the everyday blessings. I focused so much on seeing my circumstances change and wanting the victory that I wasn't enjoying my everyday life the way I could have. Victory and breakthrough are an amazing blessing from God but we should not need that in order to praise Him. ***Our praise should not be dependent on our victory!*** Don't just pray to say the words but pray with faith. Praise Him with faith. Love Him, even if you don't see the breakthrough come. Worship Him in the waiting, not just when you've received what you prayed for. And believe me when I say that your joy will be complete. We can still enjoy our lives while we wait for the victory. And by all means, when the victory does come, all the more we can jump, sing and holler in thanks to God—but while you're waiting, trusting and hoping in God to deliver you, give Him the praise, honour, glory and worship He deserves—not because you need to but because He is worthy of it all.

CHAPTER 12

Resting While You Wait

Resting in God is a gift that we are given. We didn't earn it. It wasn't something we earned by doing enough good works. It wasn't even because we deserved it. It's a free gift that God offers. He wants to shoulder the burden and let us give it to Him, while we rest and wait on Him, our Victor.

Resting is hard. It shouldn't be, but it is. At least for me it is. It involves taking myself out of the equation. It involves sitting in the back seat and letting someone else drive, without being a backseat driver. It means letting someone else take the reins when I'd rather do it myself. It's a strange dichotomy—the idea of rest being a welcome friend, yet when it's something you are forced into, you'd rather do anything *but* rest.

God calls us to rest in different seasons of our lives. I know for me, it's been hard to rest most of the times I've had to. Whether due to an injury or because you just can't keep going at the pace you have been, rest needs to happen. But why is it so hard?

The last thing you probably want to hear right now, while you're in the middle of the struggle, is: "You should just rest and wait on

God." Yeah. Okay. Sure. It's the equivalent of someone telling you to "calm down" when you're upset. Because you know, that's *always* effective in calming someone down. (Insert eye roll here.) It usually erupts with, "Calm down? Calm down?!! You want me to calm down???!!" Yeah, it's usually downhill from there.

The same is true when you're told to rest and wait on God while you're in the middle of a struggle. It's just not what you typically want to hear. You're more likely looking for active solutions to get you *out* of the problem. You want a clear path to the way *out* of the wilderness. You want to do everything in your power to just get past this. But therein lies the truth: you're probably relying on yourself. Self-reliance: as in taking care of yourself. You're so desperate to get out of this wilderness, this desert; your feet are weary, your mouth is parched, you'd do almost anything to pound out that last kilometre to the nearest Hilton Hotel and spend the rest of your days sipping ice-cold drinks by the pool. There's almost nothing you won't do when you're in pain. Any possibility of relief is a welcome subject. Why do you think there are so many products out there that claim to be the 'fix-all' for whatever ails you? There are thousands, maybe millions of them! All geared towards being 'the thing you need' to fix your problems, whether it be financial or physical or emotional. When you're in pain you're willing to try anything.

Anything but rest.

Anything but wait.

Anything but rest and wait.

Yet Scripture is full of these examples of resting and waiting on God. Take Isaiah 40:31 for example. "But those who hope in the Lord will renew their strength. They will soar on wings like eagles; they will run and not grow weary, they will walk and not be faint" (NIV).

We are reminded over and over to get out of our own way and enter the peace that comes with resting in God. The Word tells us that it brings health to our bones. That it gives us strength when we have none. That we will be as energetic as youth. I've asked myself, "How do I tap into *that*? That sounds amazing!" Yet the answer is always the same: you have to rest and wait. There's no secret, mysterious prayer formula.

I haven't sold you yet though. I know it. I know because I've been there. Too many times to count. When hardship comes in my life, my first instinct is to jump into gear and get moving on the fastest and best solution for my problem.

When you've faced disappointment, it's easy to give up on hope —period. You figure that if you choose not to hope then you can save yourself from disappointment. You're so petrified of facing another disappointment that you build up a wall around your heart. This wall started off small, only a few pebbles stacked in a row but as your hope diminished and more prayers went seemingly unanswered, your wall grew higher. You tried to tear the wall down but now those few pebbles have cemented themselves in. And like a parasite, as your hope diminished, the wall grew. Pebble by pebble, then brick by brick and now the wall that's been built around your heart is tall and thick. It wasn't meant to be permanent but now it is

—and it's strong. You built this wall to protect your heart but it has actually hurt you. It's hardened you to God's voice. Its robbed you of feeling hope. It's taken away your joy and it's given you a false sense of security. This wall—this huge wall that you thought you needed—has become a hinderance. How do I know about this wall? Because I learned that I had one, too. It had become so big that I didn't know if I could ever dismantle it but then something happened…Jesus came in and He took it down for me. He knew I was tired of the fight and tired of the disappointment so He let me sit and watch while He destroyed the wall. He didn't dismantle it brick by brick like I imagined but instead—like the wall of Jericho, He came in with one fell swoop and He destroyed the wall. He replaced the wall with a garden. A garden of rest. And He told me that this was now going to be where I could rest my heart. He placed still waters beside me and He told me to lay my head and let Him do the work while I rested (Psalm 23).

See, when you're in the midst of the battle, and you're weak, God is your strength; "But he said to me, 'My grace is sufficient for you, for My power is made perfect in weakness.' Therefore I will boast all the more gladly about my weaknesses, so that Christ's power may rest on me" (2 Corinthians 12:9). He steps in and He tells you to rest while He goes to work. He knows you need Him and He's more than ready to go to battle for you. You don't have to keep fighting. If you've come to the place where you're exhausted and frustrated, it means you waited too long to ask for God's help. It means you tried to do it on your own and didn't let God fight your battles for you. But now that you recognize that, give your battle to Him.

This verse is long, but please take a moment to really digest what it is saying because this is truth that we need to be reminded of and let it sink deep into our soul when we get into that space of trying to do it on our own. Human effort = frustration. Let God into your life to work His perfect plan out in and through you!

> "Let me ask you this one question: Did you receive the Holy Spirit by obeying the law of Moses? Of course not! You received the Spirit because you believed the message you heard about Christ. How foolish can you be? After starting your new lives in the Spirit, why are you now trying to become perfect by your own human effort? Have you experienced so much for nothing? Surely it was not in vain, was it? I ask you again, does God give you the Holy Spirit and work miracles among you because you obey the law? Of course not! It is because you believe the message you heard about Christ" Galatians 3:2-5 (NLT).

God's plans for us are good! When we are working on our *own* redemption plan, figuring our own way out of the desert, that's when we can get stuck. Suddenly you turn the corner on the path you made for yourself and you realize it's a dead end. Or even worse, you have 14 paths open up to you and now you have no idea which one to choose. Sometimes an influx of many paths is harder to deal with than just having one path in front of you.

I received some upsetting news today. The content of the news doesn't matter, but what does matter is that it was frustrating to hear that yet again, another door closed that I was hoping (in my own will) would be open. I had prayed. I had sought the Lord. I had prayed His will. Truly and sincerely. I trusted in His plan. His way. Whatever that looked like. But the truth is, I didn't fully surrender my own will. There was a small part of me that was holding out on my own design for the answer. The truth is, when the door didn't fling open and was instead closed, I defaulted to wishing He'd followed my ideal plan, the way that I thought it was supposed to happen. I was hoping that if I prayed enough for God's will, I'd please God and He would do it my way; that He'd fling that door wide open and say, "Oh, Chelsey, you genius, you. You had the perfect plan. I'm so glad I was able to follow it for you," and I'd run off into the sunset and live happily ever after. Do you ever do that? Do you pray and truthfully and sincerely trust God's will, but you've also got a little cue card in your back pocket, little flash cards to guide Him on what you think would be the best way to do it, or the best outcome? Do you trust His plan for you but when it doesn't go as you thought it would or planned or hoped it would, you wonder what on earth could be better than what you had planned?

If you do this too, you're not alone. It's human nature. It's the reason I need to continue to pray daily for more of Him and less of me. Because although it's human nature, I don't want to default to me. *I want to default to Him.* I want to get to a place where I throw my entire plan out the window and really trust His plan in whatever way He does it. I want to be there…but I'm not 100% there…yet.

Hope is like a sunrise. If you've lived any time on earth, you know that like clockwork, the sun will rise in the morning and set in the evening. You don't need faith to believe that. You've experienced it and you have witnessed it so many times that it's become natural to you. You expect it without even thinking about it. Hope is the same way. When you're first starting out, it can be hard to believe and have faith in hope. But as time goes on and you trust in God—knowing He is good—and as you see His faithfulness, that hope begins to take root. And instead of it being something you need faith for each day, it becomes routine—like the sunrise—and you begin to expect the good things God has in store for you. I won't tell you that it happens overnight. It doesn't. It takes work and practice by meditating on (practicing and reading) the Word and also prayer (being in constant contact with God). But that seed of hope will bloom and grow, just like the sun always rises and always sets.

Give yourself permission to hope again. Don't believe the world's lies that you 'shouldn't get your hopes up.' That's not what the Bible says for the life of a believer. It says all throughout Scripture to trust in God as your hope. And as I said earlier, we either choose to believe the Word or not! I choose to believe it because just like God, it's always been faithful and true. As you give yourself permission to hope again, tell God that. Tell Him that you're entrusting yourself to His will and His way. Praise Him.

Worship Him in the process. Love on your loving Heavenly Father, as He loves on you.

I am still learning to surrender completely. I am still learning that His design is better than mine. I am still meditating on the truth that His plans are good. I am still needing my mind renewed daily, to let the truth in—that He's got my problems and He's already got my solutions. Sometimes they just take time. I'm not here to figure out God's timing. He is. That's why He's God.

I don't understand it very often, in fact, I'd say only in a few instances have I really understood the reasons for God's timing but I am also not owed an explanation and that's a big part of trusting in God. If we can get there, we can begin to enter His rest. If we will rest long enough to hear His voice, peace will enter our souls. If we can listen for His peace in the babbling river or the wind blowing through the trees or the sweet birdsong, we can begin to enter that place of peace and rest. Waiting isn't meant to be hard. It's meant to refresh and restore yet we often do find it hard. It's a practice, just like anything else. You cannot plan one day that you are going to try to rest and then when it doesn't happen immediately, you give up. No, you have to commit to rest. Whether it's prayer, walking, meditating on Scripture, creative time (painting, playing an instrument), or whatever that is for you. It's going to take practice. If you feel weak spiritually, pray with a friend or someone from church. Surround yourself with others who can uphold you and pray with, and for you.

You don't have to do anything in particular during this time of rest. That is, in fact, the intended purpose. You are simply being with Him. In His presence. Listening, even if you don't always hear something. Resting in His arms that are so strong. Leaning on His everlasting arms is the best place you can be.

CHAPTER 13

Proof That God Cares
(In Case You Didn't Know)

You are worthy of love. Let that sink in for a moment. You are worthy of God's love. You question it sometimes, I know. We have all questioned it at one time or another, or perhaps frequently. You wonder what you've done that's worth anything, or what you've said that's memorable. You play through your mind all the times you've failed and messed up, like a tornado that spins and spins aimlessly. You question what you did to deserve God's love because you don't feel worthy. Your sense of self-worth spills out into other areas of your life: you question if those in your life would love you if they knew all the mess-ups you've had. You wonder if you told them, would they still love you? You're afraid to show your true to self to anyone because you're fearful that they may just not like what they see. Sometimes you wonder if you like what you see… you weigh your good from your bad on a scale and you're unsure which way the scale will tip. You wonder if you're worthy of God's love—deserving, no—but are you worthy? How can you be worthy to God, you ask, when you question your own worth? You have somehow believed the *lie* that if you're worthy, nothing bad will happen to you because you have a purpose and you're here for a reason; but if the opposite is also true (something terrible does happen to you) does that mean you don't have a purpose and you're unworthy? And then the inevitable fact is filed away in your mind: If God really cared about me, He would see my worth and purpose and protect me from any trouble. So I guess that means God doesn't care.

And there it is.

That was an example of the pattern of thinking that led you to that place of questioning if God cares for you. The question that keeps pestering your mind, below layers of denial and subconscious understanding. It began as a simple question but your mind filled in all the blanks. The problem is your mind failed you. It filled in the blanks with its own human understanding of the way things work in the world but it didn't factor God into any of its rationale. And the enemy knows how to plant and twist thoughts, too.

God isn't a schematic that we can systematically plunk into a computer program and achieve statistical answers. He doesn't operate the way the world operates and He doesn't operate the way our minds would have us believe. Mixed in with all the chaos of our thinking is the enemy who tries to convince our minds with human reasoning. When that mutual acquaintance doesn't wave at you when you wave at them, do you assume it's because they're mad at you; when in fact they just happened to not see you? Your mind immediately fills in the blanks and it can be partly human nature that assumes the worst but it can also be dependent on your mood and your level of stress. Then the enemy takes that and tries to twist it into a big rats nest of emotions.

We have this ability as humans to fill in the blanks—but often we don't assume the best, we assume the worst. It's easy to do! And it takes diligent practice to try to change that mindset and pattern of thinking. But one thing I can tell you is that that line of thinking is not going to lead you towards joy and if it's negative, it's not from God. He loves restoration and harmony, joy and peace! And when your mind tells you to think the worst of someone or a situation, you can be assured that it's not God. Have you ever come to a conclusion about a situation and asked yourself afterwards, *how did I come to that conclusion?* Life is a series of events but often our minds need to fill in the blanks to grasp the whole picture. It can be problematic when we fill in the blanks without knowing all the information or we fill in the blanks with the worst case scenario.

There are many different personalities but generally speaking we can categorize people into one of three groups: pessimists, optimists and realists. Realists say they see the situation as fact, separated from emotion and can easily predict what will happen based on that fact. However, the realist is often not assuming the best, but instead assumes the worst, citing the need to prepare themselves for the outcome. Personally, I see myself as more of an optimist and prefer to hope for the best but even as an optimist, my mind can easily fill in the blanks with a 'realist' view of things. I can misconstrue what someone said, unintentionally, or take something the wrong way and before I even consciously realize the conclusion I've reached, I've come to a decision based on very little information.

This all plays into how we then relate this same way of thinking in our relationship with God. We begin to fill in the blanks, often not assuming the best. When we don't fully grasp or understand who God is we can allow our human understanding to cloud our thinking. When we miss out on studying and learning about God's character, we cannot fully experience all that He is. We apply our way of thinking—our finite, immediate, human way of thinking—to God's vastness, not ever fully submitting to the ideal that He is more abundant and immeasurably more than we could even imagine. It is when we are in the midst of the struggle that we need to press more into experiencing and studying who God is, so that we don't allow our human perceptions to cloud the way we see Him. It's quite easy to fill in the blanks of our struggle with our own ideals of 'why.' It's easy to fill in the blanks and assume that God isn't listening or hearing our prayers because we don't see tangible change yet. It's easy to fill in the blanks with the sneaky lies the enemy tries to make us believe. But if we know the truth, if we learn more about who God is, then the truth should drown out the lies. We have to be willing to stop filling in the blanks and instead ask God to reveal the truth from the lies. We need to be willing to assess our thought life and put our reasoning on hold—or even better, divorce it altogether.

I read this quote one day and its reality and truth spoke so deeply to me. I realized that this is the message that we as believers need to hear. This is the message that is being missed in the world today. The world where Christians and churches have become brand-obsessed and wanting to keep fitting into the world, where the goal is 'follows' and 'likes' on new ideas at the expense of watering down the true gospel. We have missed the mark—completely. Because in all these feeble attempts to capture an audience, what's been forgotten—or rather *who* is being forgotten—is the one who designed it all in the first place. God.

This is the quote I read:

> "It is tempting to read the Bible as a roadmap for our lives or as a guide for 'abundant living.' But the Bible, strictly speaking, is not a book about us. From Genesis to Revelation, it reveals and celebrates the character and work of God" Jen Wilkins (Speake).

Below that quote was a commentary by Wendy Speake in which she stated, "This quote by Jen Wilkins is so counter-intuitive, even in the American church. We tend to come to life (and even God) as though we're on some treasure hunt to find all the blessings possible! But what if God is the blessing? What if a life bound up in Him, knowing Him, intimately attached to Him…is the abundant life we've been after all along? You see, the blessing is the by-product not the goal! Christ is everything!"

That truth really resonated with me and it resonated with this whole journey of struggle and hardship. We so often focus on so many other things other than the truth that God is our blessing. God is our prize. God is who we are privileged to know and as we face struggles in our lives, we can of course glean understanding and have our faith built up by the Word but if we take all the quotes and sermons away and we just look at where our help comes from, it's God. It's always God. He is the end from the beginning and He is our blessing and our prize. We have so much to be grateful for simply by knowing Him. Knowing that he calls us by name, that He knows us intimately. When's the last time you stopped and just thanked God for being God?

Protecting us on our Journey

One of the beautiful truths that God showed me recently about the beauty of how He works in our lives is that while we are in the waiting, while we are in the wilderness and while we are in the middle of the struggle, He is there taking care of all our needs. God led me specifically to Deuteronomy 8 one day. In Deuteronomy 8, it talks about how God led the Israelites through the wilderness for 40 years. In those 40 years, God took care of even their most basic needs: He gave them food from heaven, He gave them water from the rocks and even the clothing they wore did not wear out because God supernaturally prevented that. Think about that. Clothing is a need but not like water is a need or food is a need. Yet still, He took care of even the smallest details.

> "Remember how the Lord your God led you all the way in the wilderness these forty years, to humble and test you in order to

know what was in your heart, whether or not you would keep His commands. He humbled you, causing you to hunger and then feeding you with manna, which neither you nor your ancestors had known, to teach you that man does not live on bread alone but on every word that comes from the mouth of the Lord. **Your clothes did not wear out and your feet did not swell during these forty years**" Deuteronomy 8:2-4 (NIV, emphasis mine).

God showed me that He has this *same* provision for all of us as we rely on and trust in Him in the middle of the struggle. If we are constantly relying on self and not looking to God then we are not going to receive the same provision as if we are relying on God for our 'daily bread'. Although there are many similarities between this story of the Israelites' time in the wilderness, and how God operates in our circumstances, we also have the blessing of living under grace. God knows your heart and He knows when you are earnestly seeking to do His will, even if it means you make mistakes and mess up. We all do! But if our hearts are pure and postured toward Him, He knows that and in His goodness and His grace, He helps us through each of the storms and struggles we face. He takes care of our daily needs. He doesn't let a single thing slip as He promises to take care of us.

> "These Deuteronomic texts suggest that the forty years of wandering were not a punishment but rather a beneficial opportunity for the Israelites to experience God's power, when they were deprived of all bounties but still survived and even flourished" (Kugler).

This just proves to me how much God cares for both our big and our little needs. Not even the smallest detail is lost on Him. He makes sure that we are taken care of in every way possible.

Never in my lifetime have I been so keenly aware of how much God takes care of me as when I'm in the midst of a struggle. I am not saying the process is effortless but what I am saying is that I *see* God's provision for me when I'm struggling and my back is up against the wall. God draws nearer to me as I draw near to Him which is a promise that I've seen Him fulfill over and over and over again.

Have you ever noticed that? Even if your circumstances haven't yet changed, as you wait and trust in Him to bring you through it or to change your circumstances, somehow He helps you through it. Somehow He shows up in big ways. Verses that you've read 50 times are now all the sudden a fresh word. Or friends that you haven't spoken to in months suddenly text you with an encouragement. Or someone you run into tells you you've been on their heart and they're praying for you. Clearly God has helped you through your battles and trials, because you're still here. I know it's been hard but you're still here. God isn't finished with you yet and He draws nearer to you as you wait and trust in Him. He gives you the ability to get up in the morning and go on with your day. He speaks truth to you that quiets the storm going on around you. He's there. He touches you as He works on your situation. You aren't left alone to fend for yourself. You have a Way-Maker who's always at work.

"Are not two sparrows sold for a penny? Yet not one of them will fall to the ground outside your Father's care. And even the very hairs of your head are all numbered. So don't be afraid; you are worth more than many sparrows" (Matthew 10:29 NIV).

"The LORD did not set his heart on you and choose you because you were more numerous than other nations, for you were the smallest of all nations! But it was because the LORD loved you and kept the oath he swore to your ancestors that he brought you out with a mighty hand and redeemed you from the land of slavery" (Deuteronomy 7:7-8a).

You see...God chose you, specifically, not because He had to, but because He wanted to. He has a purpose for you. He cares about you, whether you accept that truth or not. He wants you to know deep down on the inside of you that you can entrust yourself to Him. He won't let you down. The entire Bible is a love story of a God who keeps forgiving and loving His children. He won't ever stop showing up with this truth.

As you wait on God to see your breakthrough, know that He lovingly cares for you and holds you close to Him. I can look back at some of the struggles I've faced and with gratitude, I can be thankful for the times when He drew so near to me while I went through the hardest points. How He never left me alone. He always made sure I knew I was loved and that He was with me. Whether it was leaving me reminders (often I would find heart shapes in the oddest places, but I knew it was God), showing me verses that He would highlight to encourage me or a friend who was praying for me. There were so many, when I look back now. God knows what you're going through. He is fully acquainted with our suffering. He knows. He cares. He holds you close to Him. He is working while you wait. I promise you, He is. Place your trust in His hands while He holds you close.

> *For we do not have a High Priest who is unable to sympathize and understand our weaknesses and temptations, but One who has been tempted [knowing exactly how it feels to be human] in every respect as we are, yet without [committing any] sin" Hebrews 4:15 (AMP).*

Misconstrued Ideas of Blessing

As much as we desire to live a 'blessed life,' here on earth, I have learned that in searching for that and trying to attain that in my own life, I was aiming for the wrong target. I thought that being free of struggle and hardships meant that God was blessing me. I believed that a blessed life is one that is full of clear skies and never encountering storms. I subscribed to the belief that if I could just get my spiritual walk figured out, God would rescue me from ever having to encounter any opposition, hardships or pain in my life; I believed that would be the evidence of a faith-filled believer's walk: problem-free.

The issue with this belief was that I was searching for the wrong treasure. I was striving first of all in my own strength but I was also striving for the wrong thing. Blessing, in our culture today, is associated with ease and often prosperous living. But we have got it all wrong. The blessing is not a struggle free life—the blessing *is* Jesus. The blessing is God and the Holy Spirit. When we focus our eyes on all that we want God to do in our lives, we are fixated on the wrong thing. We are missing out on the blessing that has already been given to us. The gift of salvation. The gift of walking through life with God. The continuous gift of being in relationship with God. That is our blessing. Healings, miracles, gifts, favour—all of those things are byproducts of a good, gracious and merciful God who loves to give His children good gifts, but they are not the blessings themselves.

When I was struggling with my health, I was fixated on receiving healing and I continually asked God to change my circumstances *the way I wanted it to happen*—in my narrow way of thinking. This doesn't mean I didn't spend time with God and rely on Him daily—because I did—but struggle is a strange thing. It can lead us to act and behave differently than we normally would because we just want the struggle to end. For me, I was looking more at what God could do for me than simply being with Him. I allowed my desire for healing to override my desire to let God be in control—to let him do what He knew would be best for me. I allowed my desire for healing to override my desire to just be with God; resting with Him, just simply being in His presence. I kept asking God to fix my problem (as I saw fit) but instead God was continually reminding me to just keep my eyes focused on Him, to trust Him and surrender control.

It's like when you put together a puzzle. You dump the box of 1000 little pieces on the table. They're tiny, full of funny shapes and similar colours. If you only look at one isolated piece, you cannot figure out the puzzle. In order to begin piecing them together, you need to see a picture of what the end result will be. If you don't have that, you will waste your time trying to guess which pieces fit together. When we focus on our problems, we are like one individual puzzle piece. Our focus is so singular on that one thing, that we cannot see the big picture. But God can see the entire puzzle and He knows what pieces belong in each spot. We have to allow Him to put the puzzle together and we do that by seeking God and only God—not what He can do for us.

God is also a God of mercy and when we call out to Him, He desires to rescue us. He is an incredibly merciful God! He does rescue us but we have to allow Him to do it the way He desires, and in His timing. Remember; He sees the whole picture.

Oftentimes, in the struggle is where we learn about all the characteristics of God; not because He always immediately rescues us but because it is in the struggle that we see Him holding us, pouring out mercy and grace upon us to endure and push through. We are given a supernatural grace and ability to endure the hardships that come and God does a beautiful thing where He then works good from that hardship and after, we see that we grew in character, and in our relationship with God. If we miss out on seeing that, and remembering that God is our blessing, we are robbing ourselves of the joy of truly knowing God.

You've reached the finish line of this book, but you're at the starting line of where you'll go from here. This is an exciting place to be in many respects. You can take the things you've learned and begin applying them to your life. But I want to pause for one last moment and share with you one of the most important principles that applies to this journey but more so to your entire life: The work that is ahead of you: let God do it in and through you. None of the knowledge you've acquired in this journey should be attempted in your own strength. That's going to lead to burnout because we simply just cannot do it all. We aren't perfect. We need God's help but that's exactly my point. Let Him help you. Put down your sword and entire battle gear and let God go to battle for you. Rely on Him to change you, do not rely on yourself for change. You cannot do what God can do. Give Him the ability to do the work He needs to do in you, and in doing so, let the pressure go. You're not doing this alone—you're doing this with the King of the entire universe.

I encourage you to read slowly through this verse and let it sink into your soul. It's one of the most beautiful, scriptural reminders of how we can apply all of these things to our daily lives, in such a practical way; by putting aside our agenda, removing the pressure of self-reliance and lifting up your worries in surrender to God.

> *"Don't fret or worry. Instead of worrying, pray. Let petitions and praises shape your worries into prayers, letting God know your concerns. Before you know it, a sense of God's wholeness, everything coming together for good, will come and settle you down. It's wonderful what*

happens when Christ displaces worry at the center of your life" Philippians 4:6-7 (MSG).

I will leave you with this. Trust that God is taking care of even the smallest details. See from His Word that He cares for you, He loves you beyond all measure and He has a good plan in store for your life. He—alone—is your blessing. *Your wilderness will not last forever.* He already has the route home mapped out for you. He's been preparing your solution and He won't ever leave you. Be encouraged in hope and "the peace of God, which surpasses all understanding, will guard your hearts and your minds in Christ Jesus" (Philippians 4:7, ESV).

Works Cited

Christie, Vance. "Giving Thanks in All Circumstances – Corrie Ten Boom." VanceChristie.Com, 22 Nov. 2016, vancechristie.com/2016/11/22/giving-thanks-circumstances-corrie-ten-boom.

Dr. Gili Kugler. "Did the Exodus Generation Die in the Wilderness or Enter Canaan? - TheTorah.Com." The Torah, www.thetorah.com/article/did-the-exodus-generation-die-in-the-wilderness-or-enter-canaan. Accessed 8 Aug. 2020.

Johnson, Bill. The Essential Guide to Healing. Chosen Books, 2011. https://renner.org/you-have-a-two-edged-sword/

Meyer, Joyce. "Joyce Meyer On." Twitter, twitter.com/joycemeyer/status/447689235269955584?lang=en. Accessed 18 June. 2020.

Meyer, Joyce. "Table Talk with Joni" *Daystar Television*, www.daystar.com/. Accessed October 21, 2020.

Murawska, Magda. "The Dangers of Comparison – Albert Ellis Institute." albertellis.org/the-dangers-of-comparison. July 31, 2014. Accessed 10 June 2020.

Renner, Rick. *You Have a Two-Edged Sword*. 6 Nov. 2020, renner.org/article/you-have-a-two-edged-sword/.

Sogunle, Kemi. Beyond The Pain: A Return to Love. Kemi Sogunle, 2016.

Speake, Wendy, (wendy_speake). "This quote by Jen Wilkins." Instagram. 9, October, 2020. https://www.instagram.com/p/CGHpYxvgDME/

www.ingramcontent.com/pod-product-compliance
Lightning Source LLC
Chambersburg PA
CBHW020905080526
44589CB00011B/450